OPEN EDUCATION

OPEN EDUCATION

alternatives within our tradition

JOSEPH D. HASSETT

ARLINE WEISBERG

Prentice-Hall, Inc., Englewood Cliffs, New Jersey

ISBN: P-0-13-637306-2

C-0-13-637314-3

Library of Congress Catalog Number: 79-37640

10 9 8 7 6 5 4 3 2 1

PRINTED IN THE UNITED STATES OF AMERICA

Prentice-Hall International, Inc., London
Prentice-Hall of Australia, Pty. Ltd., Sydney
Prentice-Hall of Canada, Ltd., Toronto
Prentice-Hall of India Private Limited, New Delhi
Prentice-Hall of Japan, Inc., Tokyo

*Photographs reprinted by permission of the photograhper,
Wendy Holmes, and Wave Hill, Inc.*

*This book is dedicated to children
and the improvement of their lives—
in and out of the classroom.*

Contents

PART II
Educational Roles

Foreword

The program described in this book is an outgrowth of Wave Hill's continuing institutional commitment to urban environmental education. In 1967 teachers from England's Nuffield Foundation Junior Science Program gave their first workshop on this continent at a Wave Hill Summer Program. From that time Wave Hill's urban environmental education has grown in many significant ways into the present Open Classroom Environmental Education approach. A grant from the Ford Foundation made financially possible the development of this innovative approach.

With the publication of this important book, the Wave Hill approach can now be offered to a wide audience. In this way its benefits can be shared freely; and the hope expressed in dedicating this book to children will be realized at least in some practical way.

THE BOARD OF DIRECTORS
WAVE HILL, INC.

Preface

If experience is indeed the best teacher, the authors have had the best teacher to guide them in the writing of this book. The approach to open classroom-environmental education presented here is the product of the authors' experience in developing a program that has been incorporated into elementary schools in four community school districts of the Bronx (D.S. 8, 10, 11, 12), in one community school district of Manhattan (D.S. 6) and in one Bronx parochial school.

The specific forms this approach has taken resulted not from theoretical constructs but from a commitment to meet the educational needs of children. Parents, teachers, principals, supervisory personnel, and district superintendents shared with the authors the task of sifting out the genuine needs from the spurious or ephemeral, and determining practical and effective ways of responding to those needs. In developing the program and in writing this book, our intent has not been to replace, a priori, the old with the new or the traditional with the innovative. Rather, our intent has been to offer old as well as new alternatives that promise the best available educational experiences for our children.

In order to prepare elementary school teachers to use the approach presented in this book, the authors focused on meeting the needs of the teacher in day-by-day classroom situations. Workshop-seminars, the bases on which this book was developed, have been planned and conducted with the realization that teachers need not only to understand clearly the objectives of this teaching approach but also need to learn how to put those objectives successfully into practice.

On-the-spot assistance in the classroom was given to teachers in the Wave Hill program to offer them the kind of help they deemed most useful. The resulting feedback regarding problems encountered provided the bases for group analyses of these problems at the weekly workshop-seminars. These discussions, in turn, led to constructive educationally-sound solutions. To those dedicated, adventurous, and creative teachers who have shared and continue to share in the shaping of the Wave Hill Center approach to elementary school teaching the authors express their fullest gratitude.

From this rather large group of teachers we must single out those with whom we worked most closely. First we would like to acknowledge the contribution of those teachers who, early in the history of the Wave Hill Open Classroom/Environmental Education Program, quickly became proficient and developed the expertise to demonstrate this approach to other teachers: Mrs. Ellen Adelson; Mr. William Bet, currently Associate Director of the Program; Mrs. Barbara Getz; Mrs. Barbara Glickenstein, presently Master Teacher and Assistant to the Director; and Mrs. Vivian Salit.

We also thank Dr. Thomas Vinci, associate professor of education, Fordham University. Along with conducting one of the workshop-seminars, Dr. Vinci is coordinator of the program at Wave Hill for Fordham University. It is through Fordham University that graduate credits in education are awarded to those teachers who successfully meet the requirements of the course.

Administrators in the community school districts with which we work deserve public acknowledgment for their courage and foresight in introducing programs that they are convinced will prove beneficial to the schoolchildren. We are especially grateful to Dr. Charles Shapp, formerly superintendent of School District 10, for his initial encouragement; and to Mr. Sol Press, deputy superintendent, and Dr. Theodore Wiesenthal, superintendent of Community School District 10 for their continual co-operation and support.

We have saved the final bouquet to express thanks to the Board of Directors of Wave Hill Center for Environmental Studies. It was here that the seeds for the present Wave Hill Open Classroom/Environmental Education Program were planted in 1967. Through the foresight of the then executive director, Mr. Edward Ames, and of the board of directors of Wave Hill the program got underway, financed by a grant from the Ford Foundation.

Joseph D. Hassett, director of Environmental Education at Wave Hill, has headed and developed the program since 1969. Arline Weisberg has been master teacher and assistant to the director for the Wave Hill Open Classroom/Environmental Education Program since February, 1970. In the spring of 1971 the program was evaluated and refinanced by the Ford Foundation. The most recent testimony (August 1971) to Wave Hill's recognition as an outstanding environmental education and teachers' center was given by the United States Department of Interior in designating it as a National Environmental Education Landmark.

In thanking all of our colleagues and dear friends at Wave Hill we wish to make special mention of: Mr. Richard A. Madigan, the executive director; Mrs. Florence Sadovsky, our dear secretary, who cheerfully typed the first draft of the manuscript from not-too-legible handwriting; and Miss Wendy Holmes, staff photographer, whose superb work is exemplified by the photos that appear in the book.

JOSEPH D. HASSETT

ARLINE WEISBERG

OPEN EDUCATION

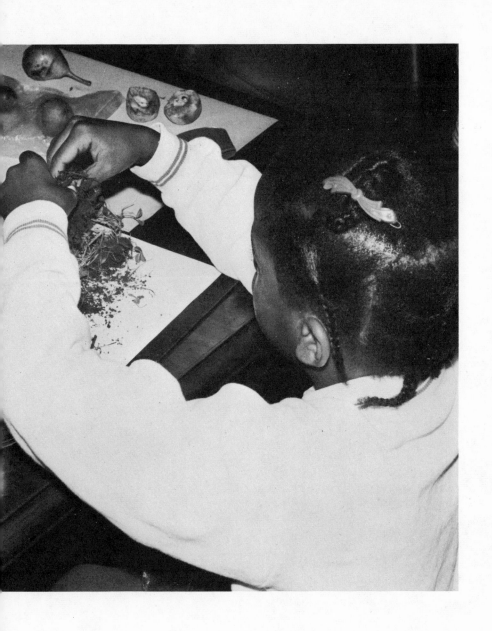

PART I

Educational Environments

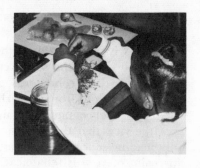

1 Open Classrooms and an Open Environment

There are numerous approaches to these fundamental questions of education: How do children learn to learn? How do teachers learn to help children learn better? How is an "open classroom" approach to learning related to the environment? What must our children learn today in order to meet the challenges of tomorrow? How involved should parents and the community be in the education of their children?

Our approach is an innovative educational program that has already passed through the experimental stage. It has been tested and found to be educationally sound, appealing, and effective with young children of all backgrounds and in all the familiar educational categories: high achiever, average, low achiever, disciplinary problem, turned off, truant, highly motivated, slow learner, exceptional.

The educational level we are concerned with here ranges from kindergarten children to the incipient adolescents in the sixth grade. For the teachers of these young children, we offer a specific and detailed program. We hope that many others will read this book as well. Education reaches its maximum effectiveness when the community, as well as the professional educators take part.

Children learn and develop within a community, not in a vacuum.

Each child is conditioned by the concentric circles to which he belongs. The family circle, the social circle of the extended family and closest friends, the school community, and the larger neighborhood community influence the child from his earliest years.

The school community is usually very important for the child. However, the view that the education a child receives from his school is the only genuine education is, to say the least, a narrow view. In the long run, this point of view is self-defeating. Without overall community support and reinforcement, the efforts of the school community would be negligible, if not entirely nullified. The contrary is also true. The more a community encourages a child's potential for learning and genuine growth, the more effective the school education will be.

Every educator, from a kindergarten teacher to a state superintendent of schools, needs to know the developments taking place. Every educator must analyze these developments, judge their merits and drawbacks, support what he finds educationally sound, and speak out against what he judges spurious. Is this way common goals worthy of a community can be established and achieved. Nothing is accomplished by a mechanical and silent acceptance of the status quo by those whose business it is to see that children of all ages receive the best education possible.

Parents should evaluate the program proposed in this book also. The increasing interest and active participation of parents in their children's education must be encouraged and reinforced. Parents now have a greater opportunity than ever to assert more decisively through local school boards their opinions regarding what their children should learn and how they should learn it. This book presents a viable alternative to the more traditional formal method of teaching. Since, in the near future, parents will have a choice of alternatives, now is the time to consider alternative educational programs.

This program is an *alternative* to the traditional method of teaching. It is not a total school program that must entirely replace the traditional method. To assert, as some people do, that the traditional method used in many schools no longer has any educational validity is irresponsible and arrogant. The facts do not warrant a wholesale condemnation of it. Competent teachers, using the more formal and traditional approach and modifying it with their own inventiveness, are doing successful teaching in the proper circumstances. Some teachers trained in the traditional method achieve very satisfactory results with it. They should not be persuaded—much less forced—to embrace this innovative method if they are convinced that they will not be able to handle it properly. No method will be effective unless the teacher feels comfortable with it. A very good method used poorly will only lead to a bad educational experience for the child.

The purpose of this book is not to promote an innovative method simply for the sake of innovation. The method we suggest has been proven to be a highly effective and educationally sound alternative to the traditional method. This method can coexist with the traditional method, within the same school and even within the same classroom. Neither the traditional method nor the method and program we propose is an end in itself. The pupil's good must always be placed first. What method in these circumstances will best help this child and these children?—this is the question that should determine the method, or the combination of methods, to be used.

This central question cannot be answered adequately without considering a host of pertinent questions, as dedicated teachers are now doing. Some of these questions are listed below.

- How does a child learn most naturally, comfortably, and progressively?
- What method should a teacher use to help the child want to learn, and to learn how to learn?
- Should the tested insights of Jean Piaget and the findings of contemporary child-development psychologists be put into practice?
- What role should materials play in the learning process? Are they a help or a hindrance? If educational materials are used (and these terms will be explained later), how should a teacher introduce them into the classroom? How can they be used most advantageously to lead children to genuine learning experiences?
- Can any of Maria Montessori's insights be adapted for use in a metropolitan public school classroom? If so, how, and to what extent?
- Is the classroom environment the only important learning environment? What about the school building, the schoolyard, and the neighborhood? What about the outdoor environment, in the sense of a park or nature center? How can these environments be used to motivate the children to want to learn?
- How should pupils be taught about environment problems? Is it possible to teach them at an early age that just as the environment acts on them they act on the environment? Can they understand that they are agents of change in the environment?
- What role should the teacher play in the child's learning process? Should the learning process be more teacher-centered than child-centered, or the reverse? What does a child-centered approach to teaching mean?
- Is it best to teach the whole class or to divide the class into interest-groups, and then to concentrate on group (or individual) problems? Is giving children the freedom to explore and discover the same as the so-called and once promoted progressive education? Or is it more like the so-called activity method promoted years ago and still used by some teachers?
- Does the open school or integrated day approach to teaching destroy classroom discipline? Is it too permissive? What does it accomplish that cannot also be accomplished by more direct and perhaps better, traditional teaching methods?
- Can the learning process in the classroom be truly interdisciplinary by having interesting projects for the children to work on? Are the first- and

second-graders too young to attempt a project on their own, especially if they are slow readers and cannot follow directions?

- What happens to content and the curriculum if the children are allowed to follow their interests and to do what they want all the time? How can the child's education develop progressively without a set graded curriculum to follow?

- How can the teacher be sure the child is learning to read progressively, is learning the proper concepts, step by step, in arithmetic, and is expressing himself properly in a classroom when the method is child-centered? If the child already knows how to learn in the early grades, how is the teacher necessary?

- How can heterogeneous and/or vertical family groupings provide a learning situation as effective as a homogeneous grouping? Are homogeneous groupings heterogeneous enough?

- By what criteria should we evaluate a child's growth and progress in the total learning process? Are achievement tests, such as the Metropolitan Tests, the most objective norm? Without a criterion like the grade level on which a child is reading, how does the teacher or parent know a child's stage of development?

- Can a teacher deviate from the curriculum and the traditional methods of teaching without running into a serious problem of accountability? What will the principal and the parents say? How will such a teacher's pupils do on the objective achievement tests?

- If a teacher is dissatisfied after seven or ten years with the results of the traditional teaching method, can he successfully abandon his former method of teaching and adopt a newer and different method? Is it worth the agony?

We have addressed ourselves to these and other questions in workshops, seminars, and with teachers in their classrooms. These are the questions we now consider in this book.

We are not presenting the British Infant School Informal method of education, although we do admire what the British are doing with this method in some of their schools. We are proposing a method specifically designed to meet the needs of the teachers and children in the elementary schools of New York City. Briefly, these are some of the salient features of this method:

1. It capitalizes on each child's natural curiosity and desire to learn about the things that interest him by providing, or allowing the children to provide, or by a combination of both, a multitude of materials and learning experiences. In this way each child can find, whether alone or in a group activity, what interests and challenges him at his present stage of development. By "materials" we do not mean manufactured educational materials, although some of these may be useful; rather, "materials" here means things found frequently in the child's environment that he wants to learn more about, or things deliberately introduced into his environment as "turn on" agents—that is, sources of motivation with many possibilities for educative projects.

2. It encourages the child toward inventive activity with whatever interests him at his own level of development. Reading, spelling, arithmetic, science, and art are not taught as distinct disciplines; instead, they are learned as instruments that enable one to attain an objective or goal. The teacher must exercise his ingenuity in setting up these situations and in preparing the various materials to be integrated.

3. It is, therefore, an interdisciplinary approach. The student, generally speaking, learns not by subject matter, but by working on projects that bring into play a number of different "school subjects." The teacher's judgment determines which approach is called for at a given time with a given class.

4. The teacher ordinarily does not teach the whole class as a group, although he may do so if he considers it helpful. Instead, the teacher has the children work on projects either as interested groups or as individuals.

5. The teacher introduces a number of materials from nature, such as animals (gerbils, hamsters, turtles, goldfish, toads) and various types of plants to show the relationship among the things of nature, both "natural" and man-contrived. Here again, the principle is to present things in their context and to have the pupil come to an understanding of relationships among things and subjects in school.

6. It brings home the importance of environment to the child by emphasizing the effect of the environment on human living and by demonstrating that we can do a great deal about making our environment better for human living.

We are not recommending the replacement of the present system with another system; rather we wish to provide another option to the current traditional approach. Our approach cannot be neatly categorized as the "open school," the "integrated day," or "open corridor" approach to teaching and learning. We quickly realized that there are as many "open school," "integrated day," and "open corridor" approaches to teaching as there are places and teachers professing to employ these methods. In this regard, we grew weary of the problem of semantics. What does one call a method that has similarities with the "British Infant School" approach, with the "open school" and "integrated day" approach, but is neither one of them nor all of them put together. We originally called it the Wave Hill Environmental Education Program, but that word *environment* caused us no end of misunderstandings. Many people understood environmental education only in the older sense of nature study, or in the newer but more restricted sense of environmental problems. To most people environment meant nature study, field trips, air, water, and waste pollution studies, or educating children to run cleanup campaigns for their school or neighborhood. We had actually intended *environment* to have its basic meaning, as explained in chapter two, which is how it has been used by John Dewey, Jean Piaget, René Dubos, and Theodosius Dobzhansky.

We built this method and program on some of the basic and tested insights of John Dewey. We also borrowed substantially from the published results of years of experiment with the Montessori method. The findings of the Froebel Institute in England and the writings of Susan and Nathan Isaacs were helpful, and we were very much influenced by the writings of Abraham Maslow, Karen Horney, Carl Rogers, Erik Erikson, Gordon Allport and William Glasser. Mention of the contemporary child-development psychologists who had bearing on the development of this book would be tedious, but a brief listing appears in the selected readings at the end of each chapter.

Is there a name for our method? No. Our one plea is not to classify it. Read and understand, evaluate and choose, adopt this method, and call it whatever name you deem most appropriate; we will be content if we have helped you to be a better teacher. Ultimately, only one thing counts: to teach our children with an open mind and an open heart so that they will learn with open minds and open hearts to grow into their best selves.

SELECTED READINGS

A rather wide selection of books has been given at the end of most chapters as further background. Some books suggested are popular in subject matter and style, some are more technical, and others are highly technical. Paperback editions, when known to be available were given preference over hardbound copies.

Books

BREARLEY, MOLLY, ed. *First Years in School*. London: George G. Harrap, 1963.

BRUNER, JEROME S. *The Process of Education*. New York: Random House (Vintage Books), 1960.

GORDON, IRA J. *Human Development*. 2d ed. New York: Harper & Row, 1969.

GROSS, RONALD, and GROSS, BEATRICE, eds. *Radical School Reform*. New York: Simon and Schuster, 1969.

HAMMOND, SARAH L. ET AL. *Good Schools for Young Children*. New York: Macmillan, 1963.

HOLT, JOHN. *The Underachieving School*. New York: Pitman, 1969.

——. *How Children Fail*. New York: Dell (3869), 1970.

MARSHALL, SYBIL. *Adventure in Creative Education*. Elmsford, N.Y.: Pergamon, 1968.

PINES, MAYA. *Revolution in Learning*. New York: Harper & Row, 1966.

Articles

FEATHERSTONE, JOSEPH. "Schools for Children: What's Happening in British Classrooms." *The New Republic* 157 (19 August 1967): 17–21.

University of the State of New York, Division of Higher Education (Albany). "Psychological Humanistic Education." *Educational Opportunity Forum* 1, no. 4 (Fall 1969).

2 You Can't Smell "Nothing No. 5."

THE MEANING AND SIGNIFICANCE OF ENVIRONMENT

As a teacher, your primary interest is in the child and how the child learns. Surely this question has occurred to you: How important is the environment of the classroom, the home, and the neighborhood, to the child and his ability to learn? I'm equally sure that you consider the environment to be an important factor. Let us explore just how important it is, and how we as teachers can use the environment to our advantage.

Unfortunately the word *environment* is as common now as the word *ecology,* and both are frequently used to signify all sorts of things. Let us define what we mean by the word *environment.* Our wish is not to legislate the meaning of the word for everyone; rather, we only want to clarify its meaning in our discussion.

The meaning given to the word *environment* here is derived from the writings of three internationally recognized experts. The first of these, Jean Piaget, is frequently mentioned in educational psychology courses in regard to his innovative work on the stages of development of the young child. In his writings, Piaget stresses the interplay between the child and his environment from the embryonic state through early childhood. In this and subsequent chapters, many of the suggestions offered have been developed not only from Piaget's own research, but also from the work of eminent psychologists who either built upon or improved Piaget's methods and findings.

An expert in a different field, Dr. Theodosius Dobzhansky, the world renowned geneticist, helped to shape our point of view on the meaning and significance of the environment with his book, *Mankind Evolving*. You may be more familiar with a book by the third expert, Dr. René Dubos whose *So Human an Animal,* written in a very pleasant, popular style has received wide acclaim. Though basically an appeal for us to awaken to the vast environmental problems that beset the earth, Dubos's book makes clear what the word *environment* should mean to us. What we mean by the word *environment* here is developed mainly from the writings of these three men. Every organism, every living thing, can only live in some environment.

This environment in which living things must exist is all that surrounds the organism, including other organisms. It is from the environment that the organism gets what it needs to survive, and also to develop through the successive stages of its growth. If the environment is unsuited or hostile to the organism and the organism cannot adapt to it, the organism dies. If a particular environment is a poor environment for this organism, or if a particular organism adapts poorly to a given environment, that organism may survive, but just barely. It will be underdeveloped and to some extent sick or diseased.

It is evident, then, that the environment acts upon the organism just as the organism acts upon the environment. The two are inexorably linked so closely that it is difficult to determine exactly where the organism ends and the environment begins. Just think, you are breathing air in and out at this moment. Your respiratory system is designed to do this. But what would a respiratory system be without air or its equivalent to breathe? The air, as part of our environment is necessary and whether the air is good or bad makes a great deal of difference to our well-being. It is equally arresting to imagine a digestive system without something to eat or drink. Though we rarely think of it this way, the food and liquid we ingest is part of the environment. The fact that our system acts upon it is obvious in the digestive process. The fact that this environment acts upon us is all too obvious to those of us who have been forced to become weight watchers.

This line of thought can be continued indefinitely. Feet need something to walk on, eyes need objects to see, ears need sounds to hear, and you can't smell "Nothing No. 5."

The particular kind of environment we are in is continuously acting upon us. The air we breathe in is not the same as the air we breathe out because chemical changes take place in the process. The kind of air we breathe in also changes us. Air polluted by carbon monoxide, sulphur dioxide, lead, and mercury can "change" us to the point of death. Fortunately we can take positive measures to clean up the air and thereby we change the environment.

So far our focus has been on some general aspects of the physical environment. We agreed at the beginning of this exploration, however, that the environment is *all* that surrounds the organism, including other organisms. Since we are preparing, then, for a consideration of the classroom as a physical environment and as a psychological, social, and instructional environment, we should concentrate here, however briefly, on the social, psychological, and instructional aspects of the environment that are extremely important to human beings.

Perhaps it sounds ignoble to speak of our fellow human beings as part of the environment, but they are. They affect us and we affect them. Furthermore it is admittedly a convenience, rather than a full expression of the truth, to consider the psychological environment apart from the social and instructional environment. Although the distinction is artificial to some extent, it allows us to pursue one line of thought at a time.

In any method of education, whether it is teacher-centered or child-centered, the teacher plays a very important role. His influence is and should be a decisive factor. Any method that undercuts the positive contribution a good teacher makes also reveals its own emptiness. Those who propose such a method have never experienced good teaching or have never seen a good teacher in action.

The right question, therefore, is not whether the role of the teacher is important. It is, rather, What is the proper role of the teacher? What kind of an influence does he wish to have on his students? With rare and unfortunate exceptions, all teachers want to have a good influence, so the difficulty is not in our good will or good intentions. Perhaps it can be located in what good and important mean to the teacher's role, which brings us to the psychological attitudes, the value system, and the behavior patterns of the individual teacher. Obviously his attitudes, values, and behavior patterns will create the psychological atmosphere of the classroom. The strict disciplinarian certainly creates a psychological environment different from the more relaxed atmosphere of the teacher who encourages internal discipline in his pupils while maintaining that amount of external discipline conducive to a good learning situation. As teachers we must recognize that the psychological environment we create in the classroom becomes part of the total teaching process. The youngster who spends countless hours in a psychological environment that is negative and destructive, despite the good intentions of the teachers and principal, will be seriously affected by it. It will affect the individual pupils in different ways, of course, but there is no doubt that it will seriously affect them one way or the other.

What we are saying then is this: First, there is a reality which we are referring to as the psychological environment of the classroom; second, it has a day-to-day pervasive influence on the pupils; third, teachers can do a great deal about creating the proper psychological attitudes in the classroom; and finally, these aspects of the psychological environment are an integral part of our overall teaching role and of the pupils' learning experience. For this reason we will devote a full chapter to this consideration later on.

By *social environment,* we mean the general interrelationship and interaction among human beings, the ways in which human beings relate to and deal with other human beings. Our own experience tells us what research in different fields of psychology and psychotherapy confirms—namely, that the social environment has a profound effect upon us. Other factors being equal, the healthier the social environment about us, the healthier we tend to be. At times we cannot control our social environment, and we must handle a destructive environment so that it will do the least harm. Frequently we can act upon our social environment to change it for the better, but this depends very greatly on our personal attitudes. Unless we try, as both individuals and teachers, to develop healthy psychological attitudes and behavior patterns, we will not be able to help create a social environment in the classroom that is conducive to human growth and self-fulfillment.

In a later chapter we will consider ways in which teachers can set the pattern for healthy social attitudes and can help their pupils develop these attitudes. The more relaxed (not dissolute), personally involved, interested, outgoing, sharing (and even loving), and possessed of a sense of accomplishment the children learn to become, the more the total environment in the classroom becomes one that in itself teaches the children healthy attitudes. It is no secret that genuine learning happens best in this kind of an atmosphere. Healthy challenges are a great incentive to the child, and they, unlike negative and destructive challenges, arise naturally in a healthy environment.

Teachers of elementary grades have to be concerned with teaching basic skills. The most basic skills are the traditional three R's: reading, 'riting, and 'rithmetic. We call them instructional skills because they are not content but are used to deal with content. They are very important means to an end, for without them the teacher cannot teach content and the child cannot learn content. If the child does not acquire good habits in their correct use, he may flounder forever in a sea of unintelligibility.

There is no disagreement about the importance of basic skills, but there is a difference of opinion as to how they should be taught. These are the questions: Is the way in which these basic skills are learned part of the overall environment of the child's learning process? If so, then on the general principle that the environment itself has a strong and pervasive effect on the child's learning process, is not the method by which the child learns the basic skills very important?

We raise these questions because the method of learning basic skills is one more feature of the total classroom environment. This we have named the instructional environment. Together with the physical, social, and psychological environment it forms the overall classroom environment. So the educational process in the elementary school is, but is much more than, a relationship between a teacher and a pupil. The total environment of the entire classroom is in itself an integral and important part of the educational process and of the child's learning experiences. In other words, the classroom environment itself teaches; it teaches behavior patterns and learning habits for better or worse. Therefore, we are deeply concerned about the environment.

"Agreed!" you might say at this point, "But are we not forgetting or neglecting to consider the importance of heredity? Certainly you cannot ignore the scientific fact that human beings have genes and chromosomes. These program our whole makeup to some extent. They are the biochemical messages that have a great deal to do with foetal and postnatal development. Aren't we neglecting this aspect of the problem?"

The answer is yes. We have been talking as if every child is the same and the environment is the only thing that matters. Heredity is certainly important too, although there are two special problems with heredity. The first is that we do not have enough scientific know-how to control the genetic factors that govern learning processes or to insure that our unborn children will be better potential learners. Science and medicine have little control over heredity, despite some recent breakthroughs. While teachers cannot do anything about heredity, they frequently can do something about the physical, psychological, social, and instructional environment of the classroom.

The second problem is that there is no way to measure with certainty the inherited, or native, intelligence of a child. Although intelligence quotient tests have a limited reliability, sufficient evidence exists to show the extreme difficulty of disentangling the dual influences of heredity and environment even at an early age. The results of an IQ test should not allow us to write off a child as stupid. (We are not speaking here of children with known brain damage or other serious physiological defects.

The difficulty of accurately measuring intelligence leads us to an insight that has immediate bearing on our work as teachers: it is meaningless to speak of heredity or environment alone. The set of genes each of us has from conception, as Dr. Dobzhansky makes clear, were affected by the environment from the first moment. The interaction between the one-cell organism we once were and the environment has been continuous. Our development through the foetal stage, the postnatal stage, through childhood and into adulthood was a development of our genes in interaction with our successive environments. Indeed, human development may even be described as the product of two interacting forces, namely heredity and environment. Messages from the genes, to use popular terminology, program the person's general makeup, but only in relation to the way in which the person acts upon and is acted upon by his environment.

The child learns most rapidly and effectively in earliest childhood, according to the findings of eminent child psychologists during the last twenty years. The research of Jean Piaget, the Swiss psychologist of whom we have already spoken, was very significant and served as a catalyst for later research in this area. Psychological studies continue to find that the period of development which is most rapid and most significant in terms of the entire life of the child occurs during the first to the fourth or, certainly, the sixth year. It has also been found that the child's environment is extremely important during these very early years.

However, you may still wish to pose the question: Which is more important, heredity or environment? Our answer, which is in accord with the scientific evidence given by Dr. Dobzhansky and other geneticists, is that the question cannot be put that way. The fact that heredity and environment are so interrelated makes it impossible to consider one apart from the other. Both are of the utmost importance. Moreover, assuming that one child is more "favorably endowed" with a specific set of genes is only an assumption and does not resolve the real issue of the heredity/environment question. To assume that a given child is more "favorably endowed" with a particular set of genes does not answer the question, favorably endowed for what? Obviously no child is favorably endowed for everything. One must be favorably endowed in relation to a chosen norm of comparison. But our task as teachers is not to judge the child according to a narrow set of norms, whatever the current ones may be, and write the child off as a slow learner or what have you. Our task is to accept the child and to help the child develop his individual potentialities.

Suppose, for the sake of the discussion, that one could speak with scientific certainty of a child as favorably endowed with a specific set of genes; this certainty would not guarantee the successful development of those genetic characteristics. Genetic characteristics develop successfully when there is a proper interrelationship and interaction of the person and the environment. This is not to say that healthy environments automatically produce healthy people; or that educationally rich environments automatically produce well-educated people. The role of the person must not be neglected when speaking of the influence of the environment. Some people are capable of coping with an environment which apparently defeats other people. We are not always sure, furthermore, what kind of an environment will be best to elicit a given person's highest potential. But we do know, generally speaking, that a child develops better in a healthy, positive, and socially accepting environment than in an unhealthy, negative and rejecting one. The importance of the total classroom environment is clear. Teachers must give their utmost attention to creating the proper physical, psychological, social, and instructional environment in the classroom.

SELECTED READINGS

Books

ANASTASI, ANNE. *Differential Psychology*. 3d ed. New York: Macmillan, 1958.

CHESS, S., and THOMAS, A. *Annual Progress in Child Psychiatry and Child Development 1970*. New York: Brunner/Mazel, 1970.

DEWEY, JOHN. *Experience and Nature*. New York: Dover, 1958.

DOBZHANSKY, THEODOSIUS. *Mankind Evolving*. New Haven, Conn.: Yale University Press, 1962.

DUBOS, RENÉ. *So Human an Animal*. New York: Scribner, 1968.

MONTESSORI, MARIA. *The Absorbent Mind*. New York: Dell (Delta 0084), 1967.

Articles

BODMER, W. F. and CAVALLI-SFORZA, L. "Intelligence And Race," *Scientific American* 223, no. 4 (October 1970): 19–29.

THOMAS, A., CHESS, S., and BIRCH, H. "The Origin of Personality," *Scientific American* 223, no. 2 (August 1970): 102–9.

3 Henry Comes as a Total Package

THE PSYCHOLOGICAL ENVIRONMENT

Visiting the classrooms of many different teachers is an enlightening experience. It is amazing how different the whole environment of one classroom can be from that of another classroom even in the same school. We are not thinking of the obvious physical differences between two classrooms within the same school, such as more space, better lighting, more comfortable desks or working tables for the children, or an advantageous location in the school building. (Most teachers are well aware of their classroom's comparative assets.) We have in mind two classrooms that have basically identical assets to begin with. When lived in by the individual teacher and his pupils, two classrooms can differ as greatly as a sunny June day differs from a rainy November day.

The psychological attitude of the teacher makes the difference. If the teacher's psychological attitude is always negative, this will be reflected in an overall negative atmosphere that will hang like a deadening cloud over the whole classroom. The classroom probably will not reflect the genuine spirit of the children, for their spirit will be suppressed by the teacher's attitude.

The opposite is equally true. The teacher who develops positive psychological attitudes in himself and in the children fosters an environment that encourages and sustains vitality, growth, and fulfillment. The teacher who tries to promote positive psychological attitudes finds himself discovering ways to improve the physical, social, and instructional environment of the classroom. Furthermore, the spontaneous spirit of the pupils will have the freedom to express itself. This freedom will truly stamp the environment of the classroom with the children's spirit.

Why is the psychological attitude so crucial? The reason is this: the other three environments (physical, social, and instructional) cannot be separated in reality from the overall psychological environment. If a teacher has a positive psychological attitude, he will inevitably create a positive physical, social, and instructional environment in the classroom. Without a positive psychological attitude, the insight, the inspiration, and the determination for constructive action will be missing. In its place will be the opposite—namely, the negative attitude of the teacher, which permeates a classroom environment and dampens the fires of insight and inspiration that spontaneously arise in the minds and hearts of the children.

Therefore let us consider some positive psychological attitudes that help to foster the proper kind of environment for ourselves and the children in the classroom. At the same time we will probably realize how we may at times fail in their achievement. What is of critical importance, however, is that we make renewed efforts to foster a positive psychological attitude, and that we renew this intention every day. It is the long run that counts, and in the long run we will gradually develop a constellation of positive attitudes in ourselves and consequently in the entire classroom environment.

A strict hierarchical order of positive attitudes is an arbitrary process we can do without. Rather, let us start with a fundamental attitude —namely, the realization that every pupil is first and foremost a human person, a *unique child different from all other children.*

When we teach children of approximately the same age level, there is a tendency to look upon the pupils in our class as members of a category. This is reflected in the way teachers sometimes speak of "my third-graders" or "my fifth-graders," or "my nine-year-olds" or "my eleven-year-olds." We may even classify the children in class when we refer to them as "pupils," which stresses their common rather than unique identities.

There is nothing essentially wrong with this way of looking at and talking about the children in our classes. It is true that they are "pupils," that they generally do cluster around an average age level, and they are members of a group that is "my class." They may also be members in categories according to grade numbers. However, the convenience of this method of thinking and talking about the children can distort our attitude. We can easily lose sight of the developing human person—the child as unique among his fellow children—when we forget he is more than the impersonal and faceless classification of "pupil" or "eighth-grader" or whatever.

Actually, the "nine-year-old" in "my class" who is "my pupil" is also "Henry." As a teacher, I will probably be associated with Henry for only one year. It is difficult but necessary to consistently keep in mind in these circumstances that Henry is not just one more like the others. Henry is a unique and developing human person. Henry is different from all the others. He is not and will never be identically like any other person. This is the wonder and the grandeur of Henry, or perhaps the tragedy of Henry, but it is Henry. Henry comes as a "package deal." I cannot choose parts of his physical makeup or his "nicer" character traits and ignore the rest. Shall I try to relate to the whole Henry and help him in every way? Or shall I hope that Henry will just be a good boy and fit into the class as an average child and not give me too much trouble? Or, worse yet, shall I try to play God and make Henry into my own image and likeness? Shall I try to form Henry into my preconceived model of what "my pupils" ought to be?

It is not easy for us to accept *as other* another human being with a religious or ethnic background different from ours, and possibly with physical characteristics, psychological traits, or behavior patterns we do not like. We do not mind that the other person is different—but only up to a point! We like the other person to be different, but only in ways that we approve, that please us, and that do not challenge us.

Ironically, we do expect others to accept us as we are, and to help us become our best selves. All too poignantly we have come to realize that we are, indeed, a "package deal." There may be physical characteristics, psychological traits, or behavior patterns that we would have parted with cheerfully at some time in our life. With maturity, we learn to accept ourselves as we are, to try to change what we can change, and to live comfortably with what we cannot change. We usually find it confusing, to say the least, when others fail to perceive us as we think we are. We feel violated when people ignore in us all that does not reflect, complement, or please them, or when we are politely (sometimes "professionally") treated "just like anyone else."

The individual child in my class, I must remember, is a sensitive human person in the early stages of development. He needs to learn to accept himself. How can he do so if his teacher does not accept him as he is? How can he feel comfortably at home in our classroom if he feels estranged or alienated, which is just another way of saying that he does not feel "like himself." How can he feel like himself if we are not accepting him as himself?

How can a teacher with thirty or forty pupils in a class seriously relate to every child as unique? Where does this teacher get the time?

How does this teacher manage to get around to each and every pupil in a class of thirty or more? Is the idea well intentioned but unrealistic?

It can be done. (The practical details will be presented in the course of this book.) At this point it is important only to tentatively assent to the fundamental principle that each child should be treated as himself in the classroom. Without this conviction, there is no reason to consider the practical ways in which this positive attitude can change the physical, social, and instructional environment of the classroom, and how these in turn can support the fundamentally positive attitude.

For example, if a teacher wishes to treat every child as a unique human person radically different from all others, then that teacher will create a physical classroom environment that reflects this conviction. (In the chapter on the physical environment we discuss many different arrangements for a classroom.) This physical environment, in turn, will help the teacher to deal with pupils on a class basis, group basis, or individual basis as he wishes. Obviously, the arrangement of a classroom has only one purpose—namely, serving the individual and collective needs of the children. The arrangement will not be a single fixed one that subordinates the needs of the children to itself. Just the reverse is true; the arrangement will be subordinated to the needs of the children.

There is an ancient expression that is apropos here: *Quidquid recipitur secundum modum recipientis recipitur*. This may be freely translated as follows: "An individual understands whatever comes to him in the manner in which he, as an individual, can assimilate it." In other words, each person comes to know and understand in the light of his total makeup and the circumstances surrounding the particular experience to be understood. Children are no different. Any experienced teacher who has taught a class with "homogeneous grouping" knows how deceptive that expression is. A "homogeneous" class of children startles the teacher with their individual differences as he gets to know them individually. Heterogeneous groupings usually reveal even greater differences in the individual children.

Consequently, teachers must not only *acknowledge intellectually* that each child is different, but must create the total classroom environment that will make this truth become a living reality in the classroom.

Recognition of every child's uniqueness is closely allied to a second psychological attitude essential for a healthy classroom environment: the necessity for the teacher to promote a good self-image in each of the children in the class. A child who regards himself as a failure or a loser, as unloved and unwanted, as dominated, threatened, and fearful, or as a member of a minority group discriminated against and foreign or whatever, brings this image of himself to the classroom. It affects his feelings, his thinking, his social attitudes, and his whole being. Whatever the teacher says or does will be received by that child in light of his

self-image. A teacher who has allowed the children in the class to engage in role playing, in uninhibited imaginative writing about themselves or others, or in expressing themselves freely by drawing themselves, members of the family, and other children, knows the influence of self-images. How remarkably children reveal their emotional attitudes and the way they look upon the world around them!

The teacher's self-image is indeed an important factor here. It helps considerably if the teacher has matured to the point where he can accept, respect, and trust the realities of himself. This maturity will be manifested by an acceptance of other human beings *as other*. It means that we must respect and trust our pupils as they are; we must help each to fulfill and develop his own self. The teacher who wants to develop a good self-image should want to help each pupil to develop a good self-image. Practically speaking, this will mean many things, but it will certainly mean accepting the other as unique and it will mean *trusting* this unique other person.

A teacher who is fearful, suspicious, and distrustful creates a fearful, suspicious, and distrustful atmosphere in the classroom. Discipline is rigid because the teacher does not trust the pupils to behave in an acceptable fashion. The children are tense and uneasy because they readily sense that the teacher does not trust them. The teacher dominates the learning process because he does not trust the children to learn to any appreciable degree on their own, or does not trust the different ways of learning that individual children have. Assignments are meticulously given to the class as a whole, with the expected achievements so tightly boxed in that a pupil can only "succeed" or be "correct" if he follows to the minutest detail the exact wishes of the teacher. This kind of teacher allows no initiative, creativity, freedom, peculiarity of learning style, or development of the child because, implicitly, he does not trust himself to trust the child. If a child does come up with an unexpected "right answer," the teacher is suspicious. The implicit assumption is that children learn and know only what *I teach them*.

Moreover to trust a child means that I must sincerely *listen* to each child. Listening attentively to each child is an art that perhaps too many teachers have not developed sufficiently. Before we can listen attentively, we must be convinced that the child has something *he thinks* is worthwhile to say and that *I must think worthwhile to hear and to understand*. How many adults are convinced that what a child says is important? Adults frequently think that, in comparison to their own knowledge and experiences, what the child has to say is objectively insignificant. But is this the correct way of listening to a child? What is important to the child is what he wishes to communicate; what he feels is important to him ought to be important to us. It is only in knowing what is important or unimportant to the child, and why the child thinks so, that we get to

know and understand the child. We must trust that he has something
he thinks is worthwhile to say if we are going to listen attentively.

But isn't listening an awful bore and a waste of time? Isn't there
only one thing that really matters in class, that is, whether or not the
child has learned what we are trying to teach him? And isn't it a simple
matter to test his knowledge with questions and see if he can give the
"right" or "correct answer"?

There is no doubt that the teaching profession and the educational
system place too much value on "right" or "correct answers." Perhaps
this is one reason why the educational process in the United States is not
considered highly successful. If a student gets a "wrong answer," it is
true that there must be a reason why. Perhaps the teacher did not approach the matter to be taught correctly. Perhaps the child was inattentive. Perhaps the matter to be taught had no meaning in the child's life,
or perhaps it was beyond the child's grasp. One could go on citing possible reasons. The most significant thing is not that the child gave an
"incorrect answer" according to some standard, but why the child gave
the answer he gave. What was going on inside the child during this entire
classroom experience? One revelatory way we can discover what goes on
in a child's mind is to let him talk while we listen to him sympathetically
and try to understand. A teacher who wants the child to learn in a way
that benefits him most has to stop concentrating on "correct answers"
and concentrate on how the individual children feel, think, and learn.
The learning process of the child and the development of that learning
process are more important than "correct answers." Teachers are aware
of the imitative and memory-retention power of the young. A "correct
answer" by no means guarantees that a child understands the matter in
question, nor does it imply that a significant learning process has happened. The child may simply be repeating by rote what he remembers
but does not understand.

Apart from those with diagnosed or genuine disabilities, children
can and will learn if they are not blocked or prevented from doing so by
methods that inhibit their innate abilities. We must trust the innate abilities of the child. We must believe that he can and will learn and will
develop at his own pace, if I, as a teacher, wish to help rather than hinder
that process. Take the matter of "failure": too often, perhaps, teachers
treat a "wrong answer" as a "failure," and a "failure" as a minor educational tragedy with no redeeming qualities attached to it. Actually a
"wrong answer" or an "unsuccessful" experiment can lead to a very
rewarding educational experience; it depends on how the teacher and
the child regard it. If the teacher has a positive psychological attitude
that considers a wrong answer or unsuccessful experiment as another
way of learning, the child does not feel defeated. Rather, the child can
feel that he has learned a great deal by discovering the source of the error

or why the experiment was not successful. This is a healthy and positive psychological attitude, and it helps to give the child a good self-image. It creates an atmosphere of inquiry and learning rather than an atmosphere of "successes" and "failures." It allows each child to be himself and to grow in learning. It is just the opposite to the tense, aggressively competitive, do-or-die atmosphere of a classroom where the most important question is "Who had the correct answer?"

To bring about the positive psychological attitudes in the classroom of which we have been speaking, the teacher must make the classroom child-centered rather than teacher-centered. To some teachers, this is heresy in its most pernicious form. It is as unorthodox as Galileo's proposition that the earth is not the center of the universe, but that the sun is the center of our "universe." It must have been maddening for people who had believed all their lives that the earth was the center to try to believe that the sun was actually the center. For many parents and teachers, it is just as maddening to try to believe that the classroom should be child-centered rather than teacher-centered. Perhaps they believe that if a classroom is child-centered, then the teacher is unimportant; or that the child is free to do as he pleases in an undisciplined and wanton way. It is most unfortunate if these are the reasons for their resistance, because it is not what we have in mind by a child-centered classroom.

The teacher is a very important and necessary person in the classroom. The natural ability, sensitivity, love of children, education, technical know-how, experience, and good intentions of the teacher have a tremendous effect upon the children in any kind of classroom. The teacher is an adult, and hopefully has found maturity through experience. The teacher should be the greatest single resource in the classroom. The child lacks the learning of the teacher, the general experience from living longer, the methods and techniques of teaching, and the authority of the teacher. There must be no confusion regarding what philosophers call the existential situation or total reality of the teacher and the pupil. There is indeed a genuine difference. The difference varies according to the levels of education and the persons who are the teacher and the pupil. But certainly there is no disputing on the elementary grade level who is in charge and responsible for what goes on in the classroom.

Any teacher who does not set up procedures to be followed, who does not instill and encourage the value of order, who does not develop internal discipline in his pupils, and does not show good class management cannot have what we mean by a child-centered classroom. A child-centered classroom does not mean chaos. It does not mean allowing children complete license to do what they want, when they want, and as they want. It does not mean permitting disorder, uncleanliness, discourtesy, unnecessary noise, aimless projects, destructiveness, or lack of discipline.

What we mean by a child-centered classroom is this: *My function as teacher is to help each child grow as best he can. But the child is a natural learner. How then can I best help each child to learn how to learn?* From another point of view, this means that I do not consider myself, the teacher, to have a body of knowledge that I must transfer from my mind to the minds of my pupils. In this latter form the teacher is the center because the teacher thinks, at least implicitly, that without him no learning could take place. The teacher is a giver here; the pupil is a receiver. The teacher is mainly active, the pupil mostly passive. The teacher presents the problem from his point of view then he proceeds to solve it; the child finally accepts the presentation of both the problem and solution and commits it to memory. The teacher demands a set way of performing each learning exercise; the pupil will be correct if he is able to repeat verbatim what the teacher has prescribed. The curriculum is so sacred and important that the teacher feels compelled to cover it, no matter how unprepared or unfit for it his class may actually be. These are some of the cornerstones of the teacher-centered classroom.

In the child-centered classroom, the teacher knows his material well but comes to class each day not to talk *at* the children from the front of the class. He comes to class as an adult and as a teacher to share with his pupils in the learning experience. He clearly recognizes their ability to learn; he trusts them, and he allows their individual differences, their styles of learning, their stages of development. He capitalizes on their individual or group interests by giving them projects that stimulate their curiosity and their desire to learn. He learns their strengths and weaknesses. He feeds their strengths with reasonable challenges, and he helps each student to improve in weak areas. He finds that he learns a great deal through his interest in and listening attentively to the students. He learns a great deal about each student: their novel ways of expression, their insights into particular problems, and their artistic abilities, among other things. Here the child is the center, and the teacher is constantly helping the child learn how to learn.

The teacher has order and cleanliness in a child-centered classroom because he explains why order and cleanliness are good, and he explains how they can be attained by cooperative action. He explains clearly and in detail what must be done, and he gets the children to accept responsibility.

Discipline is of great importance, but we are speaking of internal, not external, discipline. External discipline, though necessary at times, should not be overemphasized. We readily recognize that a child who is seriously disobedient must not be allowed to get away with it. On the other hand, external discipline can be used too freely and without significant results. It is also the quick answer for the authoritarian person-

ality and the uncertain and fearful teacher. We urge that the emphasis be placed on helping the children to learn internal discipline: the need to follow basic norms of courtesy, order, neatness, cooperation, and industry. Admittedly, this takes more time and patience. The effort is for the good and the growth of the child, however, not for the peace and security of the teacher. The basics of social living must be explained to the children, and discussions may be encouraged for them to set up the rules for cooperative classroom experiences.

Freedom is important in the child-centered classroom, but it is individual freedom without violating other people's freedom. This freedom is not license because it must be exercised responsibly. The teacher must show the children why freedom is not an end in itself, why it is a means for people to grow and fulfill themselves. While the individual child should recognize that he has a right to fulfill himself, he must recognize that others have the right to fulfill themselves too. The children should grow to accept this, and they should learn cooperative action, mutual respect, and trust. They come to realize that for any group to cooperate successfully, the members of the group must agree to common objectives and to the appropriate means of attaining those objectives. Experience shows that children learn these things, given a positive psychological environment in the classroom.

During the summer before this book was written the authors conducted a summer program for children who had finished grades one, two, or three. They were from eight different ethnic backgrounds and various socioeconomic backgrounds. Some were classified as slow learners, some as average pupils, and some as high achievers. They learned together in an accepting, trusting, warm, open psychological environment. In an ungraded type of arrangement they taught and learned from one another. The most satisfying part of it all was this: the children hated to leave at the end of the day, and even though it was summer vacation, they came gladly each day. In the evaluation questionnaire that all the parents returned to us, they universally attested to the joy and enthusiasm their children experienced during these days of genuine learning experience. They told us that the children returned home brimming with things they wanted to talk about and share with their families. One mother succinctly put it, "My child just loved every minute of it."

If education succeeds in getting a child to love to learn and to enjoy learning how to learn more, then we think it is successful. Once a child discovers the thrill of personal accomplishment and the sense of his own potential, he will be able to grow more and more on his own. And that is why we are so anxious to create the correct psychological attitude in the classroom. Without it, education becomes what it unfortunately is in too many classrooms—joyless, dull, oppressive, and fruitless, instead of the fruitful, spontaneous, exciting, and joyful experience it ought to be.

SELECTED READINGS

Books

ALLPORT, GORDON W. *Becoming*. New Haven, Conn.: Yale University Press, 1955.

ELLIS, HENRY C. *The Transfer of Learning*. New York: Macmillan, 1965.

ENDLER, NORMAN S.; Boulter, Lawrence R.; and Osser, Harry, eds. *Contemporary Issues in Developmental Psychology*. New York: Holt, Rinehart & Winston, 1968.

GINSBURG, HERBERT, and OPPER, SYLVIA. *Piaget's Theory of Intellectual Development*. Englewood Cliffs, N.J.: Prentice-Hall, 1969.

GLASSER, WILLIAM. *Schools without Failure*. New York: Harper & Row, 1969.

ISAACS, SUSAN. *The Children We Teach: Seven to Eleven Years*. London: University of London Press, 1932; reprinted 1967.

MAIER, HENRY. *Three Theories of Child Development*. Rev. ed. New York: Harper & Row, 1969.

MASLOW, ABRAHAM H. *Toward a Psychology of Being*. 2d ed. Princeton, N.J.: Van Nostrand, 1962. (Insight Book—5).

MAY, ROLLO. *Man's Search for Himself*. New York: New American Library, 1967. (Signet Q3226.)

MUNSINGER, HARRY. *Reading in Child Development*. New York: Holt, Rinehart & Winston, 1971.

PIAGET, JEAN. *Science of Education and the Psychology of the Child*. New York: Orion, 1970.

RICHMOND, P. G. *An Introduction to Piaget*. London: Routledge & Kegan Paul, 1970.

ROGERS, CARL R. *Freedom to Learn*. Columbus, Ohio: Charles E. Merrill, 1969.

Articles

FEATHERSTONE, JOSEPH. "A New Kind of Schooling," *The New Republic* 158, no. 9 (2 March 1968).

4 Classrooms Come in All Shapes and Sizes

THE PHYSICAL ENVIRONMENT

Deborah, a third-grade child, collected some tiles from a construction site and asked if she could show them to the class. Questions arose: "In which room of the completed house would the tiles be used? How could we find out?" Lynn, Laura, and Judith decided they would be interested in helping Deborah to set up experiments testing the tiles for durability, resilience, resistance to stain, and cleanability. Janet and Susan wrote to tile companies asking for information about tiles; thus they learned to use the Yellow Pages. Michael brought in some tiles he found at home and discovered that they were very different from Deborah's. Michael enlisted the aid of two other boys to perform the same tests on his tiles.

When Lynn, Laura, and Judith had results from their experiments, they found writing and recording these results to be a very tedious process. The teacher helped them to chart their findings and to present their results to the class in a clear and concise fashion. The class decided, as a result of the tests, that the tiles would be ideal for the bathroom. "How many would we need?," asked the teacher, and there was a great deal of measuring and computing. The presentation of the chart served as a turn-on agent; afterwards there were many requests for new and special ways of recording. From this single turn-on agent came science, language arts, and mathematical skills. The children did a lot of writing as they described their daily efforts in their logs. They displayed their charts on a bulletin board to share their charting experience with others. They learned how one goes about finding out new things, which is a truly relevant learning process.

Teachers respond with some of the following answers when confronted with the question, "How do you relate the environment to your classroom?" "I teach a unit on pollution"; "I motivate a cleanup campaign"; "We go for a nature walk"; or "We plant seeds in the spring." Relating the environment to the classroom involves a great deal more in environmental education than taking children outdoors or making them aware of the degradation of the environment. On the one hand, it involves creating an exciting, pleasant, motivating classroom environment for the child to work and discover in, and on the other hand, utilizing the positive elements in the child's home environment as links or turn-on agents to work towards meaningful educational experiences. To accomplish this, it is necessary to make some changes in the basic physical structure of the classroom.

Like the children, classrooms in the New York City schools come in all shapes, sizes, and many models of arrangement and décor. The environment of the classroom usually reflects the personality of the teacher operating within. Is the room dark and gloomy, or bright and cheerful? Cramped or comfortable? Formal, rigid, and regimented, or informal, flexible, and at ease? Is the housekeeping meticulous, casual, or even sloppy? Sad to say, the average classroom rarely reflects the personalities of the *children*. A classroom empty of children usually furnishes many clues about the curriculum content being covered and about the life style of the teacher, but few clues to the life styles of the children "learning" in this classroom. Can the focus be shifted so the classroom reflects more of the children and less of the teacher? Does the process of altering the physical environment of the classroom ask for an accompanying alteration in the personality of the teacher? Can this change be construed as a threat to the teacher and to his or her position in the classroom? The change that environmental education involves is a slow growth toward a child-centered learning environment without an accompanying threat to the position of the teacher. The teacher moves slowly as she gradually understands how children learn.

One way to begin this process would be to start with one corner of the room. Designate that area as the "child center," the "discovery area," or the "project area." If no corner is available, then a space marked off by a table, a large cardboard carton, or an unused easel would do for a beginning. (See Figure 1.) Discuss with your children the kinds of materials they like to "mess about" with. Observe the things they bring to school or carry in their pockets and brainstorm the learning possibilities of these objects. In the lower grades it is fruitful to begin with a pile

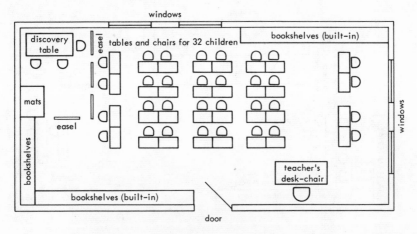

Figure 1

of "junk": boxes, bags, cardboard rollers, bits of colorful fabric, wood shavings, sticks, scissors, or paste. See what kinds of things the children fashion from these objects. Give the children space to display their projects and time to talk about them. Furnish the children with a way to record the details of the various projects. Set aside a specific hour each week for a specific number of children to work in the discovery area. Choose a time when the entire class is working on individual work or programmed instruction or a quiet activity. Train the children to use the area and stress "Take care, clean up, and share."

As the children begin to use the materials creatively and to become involved in projects, they will spill out of the area into other sections of the classroom. They will need more room to work, to store unfinished projects, and to proudly display accomplishments. By this time the teacher is also more comfortable with the change that is taking place and he is no longer threatened by the gradual alteration of his physical surroundings. The classroom must be rearranged to allow for more freedom of movement and more child-centered areas within the confines of four walls. It is possible to create flow, interest, excitement, and privacy within the four walls of the classroom, and still maintain a classroom in which traditional programs can coexist with environmental education.

Most of the space in the traditional classroom is taken up by the desks and chairs. Is it absolutely necessary, or even desirable, to have a desk and a chair for every child to use for the entire day? It is only necessary if the teacher is committed to keeping all of the children confined to their seats all day. Perhaps half the tables and chairs can be used to form interest centers in the four corners of the room, with bookcases, easels, or panels as dividers. Perhaps there can be a reading corner with mats on the floor, and an art corner with paper runners that can

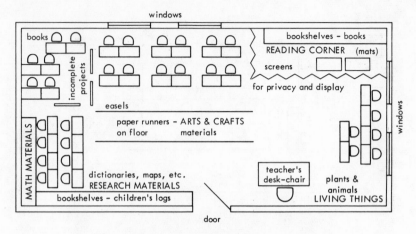

Figure 2

be disposed of at cleanup time. (See Figure 2.) Most of the New York City classrooms are provided with movable furniture that can be used for a variety of purposes in the course of the day.

When the need arises for drawing the entire class together for a sharing period or to teach a particular skill, it is a fairly simple matter to pick up the paper runner in the center and gather the chairs and mats to the center of the room. If writing is necessary, inexpensive clipboards serve as a writing surface and help children keep their papers together until they are ready to transfer them into a notebook or an envelope. A clipboard with a string fastened to it (so it can be hung about the child's neck) serves as a portable writing surface and leaves the child's hands free to work on his project.

Bulletin boards should reflect the work of the children in the classroom. During a sharing period, the children may discuss and determine which samples of the work are worthy of display on the bulletin board. Putting up a bulletin board composed entirely of the children's efforts is an excellent experience for the children. Is the bulletin board pleasing to the eye? Is it attractive? Does it tell a coherent story? Does it reflect our best work? These are all questions that children from grades one to six can learn to make judgments about. In one of our sixth-grade classrooms with no bulletin board space, the children display their work on clotheslines strung across the room, high enough not to interfere with classroom operation but low enough to attract the eye of any visitor.

At first glance, some classrooms seem to present insurmountable obstacles in their physical setup. A classroom painted battleship gray with desks and seats nailed firmly to the floor in rows presents a grim environment for children to learn in. In one such case, the teacher has learned to use mats and paper runners on the floor. The one movable table in the room is supplemented by large corrugated cartons upended to form tables. These same cartons serve as storage bins at the end of the day. The dull gray walls are covered with artwork, pictures, charts, and examples of the children's work. Mobiles hang from the light fixtures and plants bloom on the windowsills.

In the crowded New York City schools, some teachers share rooms with other teachers, and materials may not be left out. Vandalism is rampant in many schools and security is a problem. However, teachers who are committed to improving the physical environment of the classroom have improvised methods of storing materials. Some have requested school money for a steel locker with lock and key. One young teacher uses the trunk of his car for a storage area and takes his children's precious projects home each night. As we have stated before, there is no physical arrangement that is "best" or suited to the majority of teachers. Each teacher must find the arrangement that enhances his own teaching style.

Some teachers prefer to start the change in the physical environment with a small corner and gradually branch out; others prefer to start with the entire class at once. One of the teachers in our workshop arranged his tables and chairs into four groups of eight children each. (See Figure 3.) Based on his observations of the children's interests, he collected four different groups of materials: group 1—tangram puzzles, protractors, Cuisenaire rods, task cards; group 2—fabrics, dyes, detergents, bleaches; group 3—various size pieces of wood, tools, nails, how-to books for making things; group 4—geoboards, pattern pieces, shapes. Each group of eight children formed an interest center. The tables and bookshelves were filled with scales, thermometers, measuring devices, writing materials, paints, rulers, empty jars and bottles, books—in short, basic materials that a child might need to pursue an interest or complete

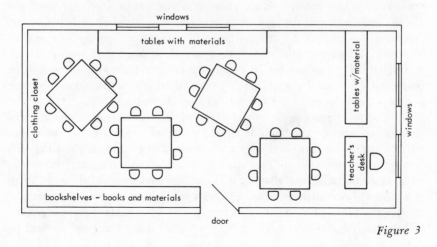

Figure 3

a project. One of the first topics of discussion with the entire class was techniques for communicating while keeping the noise level down. The children devised an elaborate set of signals. Certain pupils were elected to alert the others when the noise level was getting too high. Each day a short discussion period was held to evaluate the day's work.

An open classroom must be a well-organized, well-disciplined unit. The housekeeping must be meticulous, and the children must participate in the organizing, the disciplining, and the housekeeping, or there is danger of a disintegration into chaos. When I walk into a second-grade class and see no evidence of the teacher, with the class unaware that the teacher has stepped out to get some supplies, and every child in that class is busily at work at some meaningful activity, I know that this did not happen overnight. Children must be taught to respect materials and to use them properly, profitably, and economically. It should be made clear to them what they may and may not do with the materials provided. The rubber bands provided for the geoboards may be used to make patterns on the geoboard, or in a construction project, or in a scientific experiment, or as a sorting aid. They may not be used as weapons to annoy other children. Every material in the classroom should have a definite place. In a classroom that uses the bookshelves for storage, different colored paper circles are pasted on the shelves to mark off areas. As each material is taken out for use by the children, a small paper disc is pasted on it so that its storage area is immediately apparent. Boxes that contain many pieces of a set are labeled with how many pieces are contained. All the labeling is done by the children, and it soon becomes a habit to label and color code each new material.

Cardboard cartons are used for storage in another classroom. Each carton contains the materials for one interest area and is so marked; for example, "weather-measuring materials," and "playground-construction materials." The interest areas change as the projects change, and new labels are easily substituted. The children are divided into teams, and each team is responsible for the cleanup and proper storage of one interest area. When the children have a say in arranging the room and in setting up the routines for its maintenance, a well-organized room is relevant to the completion of their projects. In this setting they are more eager to participate in the cleanup of *their* room.

The most important initial element in the success of the environmental education approach is the selection of the materials. How does the teacher ascertain what specific materials will turn on the thirty-four or thirty-five different individuals who challenge his creativity every day? The first and most obvious way is to get to know your children. With the younger children, discuss their interests with them, observe them at play, notice the kinds of things they bring to school and carry in their pockets. With the older children, circulate a questionnaire designed to find out what their leisure-time preferences are, and what their aspirations are. Take note of things they are playing with in the desk as they *seem* to be listening to the social studies lesson. If tiny model cars turn on second-grade Johnny, then consider what other materials might be grouped with model cars to lead Johnny into a learning experience. Perhaps some clay to build a road or blocks to build a bridge might help him learn how people travel in a big city. In a fifth-grade classroom that uses model cars as a turn-on, some of the children might be interested in exploring pollution, advertising campaigns, or motors. The turn-on agent is the bridge from teacher to child. Exploration of the turn-on agent leads to the development of learning experiences.

Although the turn-on agents will vary with the age level and academic level of the children, certain materials have proved to have universal appeal. Most children, regardless of age or reading ability, respond to an animal in the classroom. There is a wide variety of animals to choose from, and the care of an animal is an educational experience.

One sixth-grade class adopted a guinea pig. They looked up the history of the guinea pig and located the guinea pig's indigenous areas on the map. One group avidly read about the care and comfort of guinea pigs so they could provide him with an adequate home. Another group weighed, measured, and listened to his heartbeat to make sure he remained in good health. Rusty the guinea pig became the inspiration for drawing, creative writing and, ultimately, a film. The children were motivated to investigate other animals. The class concern for the guinea pig involved all the disciplines—reading, mathematics, social studies, science, hygiene, art, and group interaction.

Construction materials and tools attract many children. Building is an activity with a very definite foreseeable conclusion, and it affords a good feeling of success when the project is complete. Along the way it requires creativity, reading directions, proper handling of tools, measuring, and making judgments. The completed construction may then lead to a new interest; for example, the finished table can serve as a base for a puppet theater, or the counter for a rock sale.

Odd bits and scraps of fabric, paper and string, grouped with paper bags, sticks, odd socks, paper plates, and other materials from which puppets can be constructed, may lead to a variety of skills and interests. Many children will verbalize more readily behind the mask of a puppet. The development of language arts skills is increased through the writing and dramatizing of puppet shows. Scenery adds a new dimension to the activity. A modern scene, a scene of long ago, a scene in a foreign country, these make social studies live for the child. The researching and copying of different kinds of costumes help him to become aware of how other people live. Role playing is an effective tool in helping children play out some of their aggressions.

Other teachers have successfully used spinning tops, rocks, shells, macaroni, and foreign money as turn-on agents. These may not necessarily interest your class. Perhaps something that is your hobby will be successful with your children because of your own enthusiasm. Think of the learning experiences in learning how to cook or to sew, in collecting stamps, making pottery, or raising tropical fish and you realize that you have the entire environment to draw from.

Once the teacher has observed her children and selected her materials, there is an operational sequence that has proven helpful in many classrooms. In the workshops, we call step one "helping your children develop a rapport with materials." The second step is "brainstorming the materials." This process enables the teacher not only to be aware of the educational possibilities of the turn-on agent, but to be prepared with questions, supplementary materials, and suggestions to help the children in their explorations.

Let us now consider a hypothetical situation. A fourth-grade teacher has arranged her room so that she has space for three interest areas. After observing her children, she has decided upon model cars, sand, and fabrics as possible turn-on agents. Her second task is to investigate these materials herself and to brainstorm all the learning experiences she can imagine. This process of brainstorming is one of the most valuable tools in the use of this method. As you work with a material such as sand, let your mind associate freely with all the possibilities involving sand. No matter how farfetched or ridiculous some of them may sound, make note of all the possibilities. Then group your possibilities into areas of exploration; some will be discarded as improbable, some as too sophisticated for the grade level, while others will lend themselves to grouping or clusters. These groupings or clusters are leads to the kinds of questions you will ask, the kinds of suggestions you will make, and the kinds of supplementary materials you will select. Practice brainstorming. It is a valuable activity for any kind of teaching. The three charts below are examples of the brainstorming process (see Figures 4, 5, and 6).

This brainstorming and elimination process enables the teacher to anticipate the problems, to prepare other materials to group with the turn-on agent, and to prepare questions and activity cards to guide those children who need a great deal of direction. This final chart, which we call a flow chart, is only a guide, not a rigid plan. Some of the flow areas will be discarded as uninteresting or unsuitable to the age level of the children. Some children may go off in a totally unanticipated direction, and the teacher will have to expand her thinking to include their needs. The flow chart also enables the teacher to provide for books, an integral part of each interest area.

The teacher is now ready to take the third step, to introduce the materials to the children and review the routines and responsibilities for

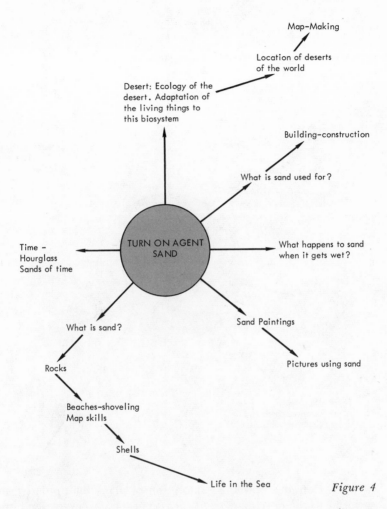

Map-Making

Location of deserts
of the world

Desert: Ecology of the
desert. Adaptation of
the living things to
this biosystem

Building-construction

What is sand used for?

TURN ON AGENT
SAND

Time –
Hourglass
Sands of time

What happens to sand
when it gets wet?

What is sand?

Sand Paintings

Rocks

Pictures using sand

Beaches–shoveling
Map skills

Shells

Life in the Sea

Figure 4

using them. A time limit should be set for the initial experience, providing enough time for the children to choose an area, become acquainted with what's available, start to "mess about," and go through the routine of cleanup. At least twenty minutes time at the end of the session should be provided for calling together the entire group and evaluating the experience. Many clues to a more satisfactory experience the next time will come from the children themselves.

"But," says the first-grade teacher, "this is no help to me. My children cannot read, they are not mature enough to make judgments, and they need constant direction. It will never work." How shall we deal with this problem? Think in terms of some of the concepts we want the first-graders to develop: light/heavy, hard/soft, bright/dull, colors, size, and

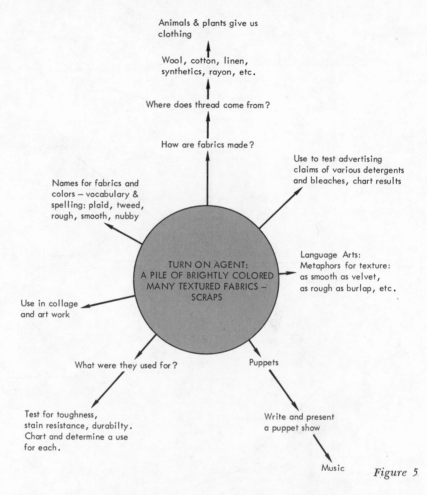

Animals & plants give us clothing

Wool, cotton, linen, synthetics, rayon, etc.

Where does thread come from?

How are fabrics made?

Use to test advertising claims of various detergents and bleaches, chart results

Names for fabrics and colors — vocabulary & spelling: plaid, tweed, rough, smooth, nubby

TURN ON AGENT: A PILE OF BRIGHTLY COLORED MANY TEXTURED FABRICS — SCRAPS

Language Arts: Metaphors for texture: as smooth as velvet, as rough as burlap, etc.

Use in collage and art work

What were they used for?

Puppets

Test for toughness, stain resistance, durabilty. Chart and determine a use for each.

Write and present a puppet show

Music

Figure 5

number. Consider how the exploration of many manipulative materials can lead to the development of these concepts. A cup of sand and a cup of water on a balance scale, bits of colored fabrics pasted on a collage, and tiny cars running through a street of blocks are valuable activities; a first-grader can learn the meaning behind these concepts from experience. A young child learns by repeating a process over and over again. If the materials are readily available, the child may experiment until he himself is satisfied that he understands enough to verbalize about what he has experienced. Then picture books can be made, articles labeled, and experiences acted out.

On a table in a first-grade classroom there are various-sized magnets, paper clips, clothespins, corks, pins, thumbtacks, plastic discs, buttons, and fasteners. A pan of water is also provided. Children can experiment in several directions. They can find out which objects sink and which ob-

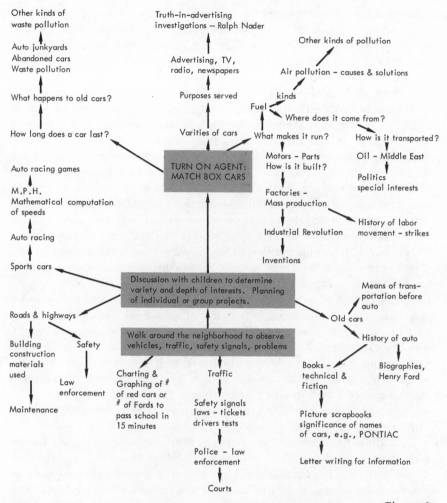

Figure 6

jects float. They can investigate which objects are attracted by the magnet, or if the magnet pulls through water. If some children choose to tell about what they have experienced, the teacher can incorporate their observations into an experience chart. Others who prefer to draw about their discoveries can combine their drawings to form a short picture book, and the teacher may help with writing the captions. Still other children may elect to demonstrate or act out their experiences.

There is a distinct possibility that the initial turn-on materials may not produce the desired outcomes. This indicates not a failure of the method, but a misjudgment on the part of the teacher. Perhaps these particular children need materials more relevant to their daily environment or their own individual personalities. A walk around the neighborhood or a discussion of the objects the children carry in their pockets might prove fruitful. Perhaps these children would be intrigued by something totally *alien* to their environment, such as a telescope or an iguana.

If the child is to have freedom of choice, and if the motivating materials are to foster valuable learning experiences, then a great variety of materials is necessary. We are aware of the cuts in the educational budget, and we have fielded many queries from teachers and principals. The most common question is, "Where can I get materials?" The school building itself is a gold mine of materials. We walk through building after building and see shelves of supplies covered with dust. Your first source of supply is your school: the science materials in the closet, the arts and crafts materials, paper, paste, scissors, string, and the standard math materials. Another source of supply is junk: egg cartons, fabric scraps, boxes, jars, paper rollers tubes, broken clocks, radios, and so on. One teacher sends a "treasure-hunt" note through her school once a month and is deluged with supplies. "I am looking for empty spools, paper-towel rollers, pop sticks, and empty jars." Free and inexpensive materials available are listed in booklets in the school library. A teacher's parents can be helpful, especially if they work in factories, and might supply scraps of wood, leather, and Styrofoam packing materials. Become a saver and a collector. A construction site or a rubble heap in your neighborhood may be a valuable source of materials and deserves investigation. You may discover something as interesting as the tiles Deborah brought into her third-grade classroom, which led to an entire project.

Purchase basic items when money is available, such as a good spring scale, balance scales, and a terrarium. Catalogs from the suppliers of school materials are invaluable. They not only provide ideas about the potential use of materials, but many of the materials can be duplicated by the children themselves using available scrap materials. Upper-grade classes can construct balance scales for use by the entire school. One very enterprising teacher removed the "rockers" from an old rocking chair and used them to construct two balance scales for her class. A wire coathanger and paper cups make a simple balance. The construction of the material itself is a learning experience. It requires planning, following directions, and trial and error. The classroom should become a workshop in which each child is encouraged to try his powers and develop his skills. Trial and error becomes a positive experience because the child has an opportunity to learn from his failure and try again.

A great source of materials is the outdoors itself. (See chapter 3.) The physical environment of the classroom may be enclosed by four walls, but the children must learn to envision their environment as encompassing all of nature, all of the neighborhood, and all of the home. We extend the physical environment to include these elements by having the children bring in materials from home and from the neighborhood. To balance the confines of the neighborhood, it is periodically necessary to take the children to other environments—for example, the ghetto child to a "natural area," to collect materials and impressions that can be brought back into the classroom and investigated further. How can the inner-city child envision what life was like when the Indians roamed New York City if he has never had the chance to explore the ecosystem of a natural area? Pictures and words won't do it, but walking in a dense growth, finding wild berries, and coming upon small animals will help to convey the impression to his senses.

Teachers have often said, "But you don't know my children. Changing the physical environment of the classroom will make them insecure. They will become disruptive. I have children who won't do one thing unless I keep after them. The children will fight and steal." No one denies that these problems happen. They occur in any method of teaching. But we would like to add one very essential ingredient to the school situation, and that ingredient is trust. Trust in the natural curiosity of children; trust in your ability to help them into new routines; and trust in their ability to learn, given the right stimulation. Get out of their way for part of the day and trust that they will choose some activity on their true level of operation, and from there you can guide them forward. Aim for the kind of physical environment that allows not only individual differences in ability, but also individual differences in personality. Give them a controlled opportunity to deal with their aggressions, hostilities, and antisocial traits in the classroom.

Environmental education necessitates a gradual physical change in the classroom environment. The goal is to move from a teacher-dominated physical environment to a child-centered one. Take a good look at your classroom, note its limitations, but don't let them stop you. Focus on the areas possible for interest centers. Explore the interests and capabilities of your children. Discuss with them the routines and responsibilities for working in a new way. Select your turn-on agents and brainstorm them. Gather your materials and let your children try the new method. Evaluate with your children the effectiveness of the first trial and improve with each successive discovery period.

SELECTED READINGS

Books

BERNARD, HAROLD W. *Psychology of Learning and Teaching.* 2d ed. New York: McGraw-Hill, 1965.

DEWEY, JOHN. *The Child and the Curriculum* and *The School and Society.* Chicago: University of Chicago Press (Phoenix Book P3), 1956.

GAGNE, ROBERT M., ed. *Learning and Individual Differences.* Columbus, Ohio: Charles E. Merrill, 1967.

GROSS, R., and MURPHY, J. *Educational Change and Architectural Consequences.* New York: Educational Facilities Laboratory, 1968.

PIAGET, JEAN. *The Origins of Intelligence in Children.* New York: Norton, (N-202), 1963.

ROGERS, VINCENT R. *Teaching in the British Primary School.* New York: Macmillan, 1970.

SCHULMAN, LEE S. *Learning by Discovery: A Critical Appraisal.* Chicago: Rand McNally, 1966.

SMITH, LEE L. *A Practical Approach to the Nongraded Elementary School.* West Nyack: Parker, 1968.

THELEN, HERBERT A. et al. *Classroom Grouping for Teachability.* Chicago: University of Chicago Press, 1967.

YEOMANS, EDWARD. *Education for Initiative and Responsibility.* Boston: National Association of Independent Schools, 1967.

Articles

Innovations in the Elementary School. The Report of a National Seminar sponsored by the Institute for Development of Educational Activities, Inc., Dayton, Ohio, 1970.

FEATHERSTONE, JOSEPH. "Report Analysis: Children and Their Primary Schools." *Harvard Educational Review* 38, no. 2 (Spring 1968) 317–28.

5 Indoors Leads Outdoors and Back Again

THE MAN-MADE AND NATURAL ENVIRONMENT

There was a famous preacher, a revivalist, who attracted a large following in the New York and Philadelphia metropolitan areas during the thirties. Known as Father Divine, he had a mellifluous speaking voice and a flair for oratory. There were times, however, when Father Divine lapsed into some humorous redundancies. On one such occasion, Father Divine was eloquently developing the theme of God's infinite attributes when he exclaimed, "And so, my dear people, let us really realize that God's ubiquity is everywhere."

I read about that incident many years ago and found it quite amusing. It came to mind again recently when I was pondering the meaning of the environment. I began to suspect that *the* environment is everywhere. Of course, the meaning of *the* environment can also be as limited as one likes in a context. But in its broadest sense, *the* environment is at least our whole earth.

Fish in streams, in rivers, and in the depths of the oceans are all in an environment. Where does one mark the end of the stream environment when the stream flows into a river? Where is the end of the river environment if the river—especially if it is an estuary—flows into an ocean harbor? Animals, flying and crawling things, jumping and walking bipeds and quadrupeds, all are in environments. The infinite variety of growing things we know as the vegetative life abounds in various environments. But where does the desert environment end and the environment of the fertile valley bordering the Rio Grande River in New Mexico, for example, begin? Human beings and their communities in villages of primitive huts, in towns of wooden frame houses, in cities with towering elongated structures of steel and concrete, these are all in certain environments too. Where does the city end and suburbia begin? Where does suburbia end and the country begin? What are the boundaries from farm land to woodland to wilderness? Does the air obey the signs that state where the city limits end, or where the state boundaries end? Environment is everywhere, so to speak, because boundaries are artificial.

Environment is everywhere we go in our normal lives. Maybe this is why we usually pay so little attention to the factors that make up the particular environments we are in at different times. We do concentrate on the environment, however, when something annoys us, pleases us, or is of special interest to us. The environment, like a comfortable, familiar suit or dress, goes mostly unnoticed. We take for granted the air we breathe, the pressures on our bodies, the surfaces we walk upon, the windows we look through, the roofs that cover us, the sun that gives us light and heat, the entire continuing miraculous process of nature itself, which we call the life cycle. Let us examine in more detail the unending ability of nature to renew itself.

Through the somewhat mysterious process of photosynthesis, the energies of the sun, captured by a plant, transform chemicals absorbed from the earth and the air into living molecules, which form the building blocks of an organism. We say that plants are autotrophic. They alone produce their own sustenance; they are the sole "producers" in nature. That they use nonliving material and the energy of the sun to grow and reproduce is evident. Unlike animals and men, however, plants do not consume other living things in order to survive. Human beings need to ingest plants and/or animals in order to grow and to continue their life over a period of time. Animals feed off other animals and/or plants. However, the animal kingdom is ultimately dependent upon plant life; therefore, plants are the sole producers. The food chain of human beings and animals is essentially dependent upon plant life. The food chain biologically begins with plant life, but that is not where it ends. To complete the life cycle we must consider the "decomposers," meaning the decaying matter that returns to nature in the breakdown of organic substances, the wherewithal to sustain the total process of life itself by completing the circle.

Therefore, the extreme importance of plant life and the photosynthetic process in the life cycle should not be taken for granted. Plant pathologists have been amassing scientific data through laborious and painstaking research not only on the photosynthetic process itself, but on the deleterious effects of pollutants on plant life and their interference with the photosynthetic process. Our attention has also been called to the shrinking wilderness, our rapidly dwindling acreage for farming, our bulldozing of green belts, and our wasteful abuse of forests. Streams and rivers have been wantonly polluted. Solid waste in every form, from garbage to abandoned cars, is piled high in the most unexpected places, while glass bottles, aluminum cans, and plastic containers are strewn along roadsides and empty lots.

What has happened? Are we so unconcerned with our particular environment that we are unconcerned about *the* environment, which includes the life cycle itself? Such an attitude may lead to the destruction of man himself. Meanwhile, the quality of the environment lowers as human beings, the so-called rational animals, steadily violate the basic laws of nature by neglecting the environment. No matter where we are, if we neglect *that particular* environment, we also neglect *the* environment. One environment extends into the next environment; all of nature is basically one. Indeed, man is different from animals, plants, and inorganic matter, but his life is intimately bound up with the inorganic, the plant, and the animal, and each is interdependent and bound up within the whole of nature.

Why then do we tend to separate our environments so artificially? Does this separation of environments, combined with our general unconcern for *the* environment, create erroneous notions in the minds of growing children? This compartmentalizing of environments along with a general indifference militates strongly against our children coming to a necessary awareness of the importance of the environment. How can children become sensitive to environmental problems if the adults generally ignore the relevance of the environment in which education itself takes place?

We touched upon some aspects of environmental education in the previous chapter, but we are convinced that very little attention is paid in the total educational process to the environments in which education is supposed to take place. Although the movement to remedy this defect has gained some momentum, most teaching by and large takes place without any significant relation to the place—the environment—in which it is taking place. Yes, most teachers are conscious of the necessity of adequate lighting, ventilation, and heating, of the necessity of chalkboard space and basic teachings aids, and things of that sort; but few use the environment of the classroom, the school, the neighborhood, the city, and the metropolitan area as concrete, practical, meaningful, and intimately relevant parts of learning experience. Let us consider first some possibilities within the classroom itself.

You are teaching a second-grade class. You wish the children to do some work in arithmetic. You want them to use numbers and units of measurements in such a way that they can form meaningful concepts. We know that concepts are abstract. They are genuinely useful and have significance only when derived from concrete experiences. Instead of having the children deal with abstract numbers and abstract units of measurement, why not use the classroom itself to do some concrete math? Why not have some of the pupils (if interested) measure their desks; others, the floor space in the room; others, the aisles between the rows of seats (if you have a formal seating arrangement); others, the height of the wall up to the windowsill. Use nonstandard units of measure, such as pieces of string, unifix cubes, or pop-it beads. These activities can then lead into the use of standard measures.

Continuing this line of investigation with the use of an ordinary bathroom scale, you can have some of the children register the weight of members of the class or the weight of a pile of books. First have the children estimate how much they weigh, because children find it a game and fun to estimate.

The same procedure can be adjusted to the interests and needs of older children. A scale map, for example, can be made of the classroom, the schoolyard, or the school building. An overall project could be a series of scale maps of various parts of the school building along with discussions as to whether they are well designed for current needs. Some children might be encouraged to draw to scale their own plans for an ideal classroom, schoolyard, cafeteria, or gymnasium. Or the class, working in groups, might design on an overall plan for a new school building. The amount of mathematics, science, and general learning that would result from such a project is not only more than results in conventional teaching, but most important, it is the result of the children's own learning process. It is truly their learning, and not something they memorize because the teacher says so.

It is April. The sun is shining through the partly opened classroom windows. Do you take advantage of this *real* learning situation?

What changes are noticeable in the classroom itself? The clothes the children are wearing? The windows opened more widely? The warmer rays of the sun? The angle of the sun? Any flowers in a window box in the classroom? Are the birds more active, if there are any in the vicinity of the classroom windows? Is the heat shut off?

What changes have the children noticed in and around the schoolyard? Are there any trees there? Have they blossomed? Why do trees blossom in spring? Why is the air outside warmer? Would the grass be growing again in the parks? In the country? Besides sun, what else do plants need to grow? Where does rain come from?

It is now winter. You are teaching a fifth-grade class. The heat is issuing from the warm radiators in the classroom. Have you, the teacher, ever stopped to ask yourself what kind of heating system is in the building? Why not start a discussion with your pupils? Ask them if they know what the various kinds of heating systems are, such as steam, hot water, and electrical convector? What are the basic principles of applied science in each system? Which do they think is the better system and why? What kind of fuel is used in hot-water and steam-heating systems? What type of pollution is caused by coal, oil, and gas? To produce electricity, what type of fuel do power companies use? Why don't they use more gas? Where does the coal, gas, and oil come from? Some teachers may quibble that they don't know the answers to these questions themselves. This argument has no bearing, though, because we are presupposing that a teacher does not want to lecture to the pupils, but wants them to be interested and prompted to do some reading and research. Furthermore, some of the children's parents have such knowledge and would be very proud to discuss these topics with your class. Industrial companies frequently will send a member of their professional staff if the students write a letter showing interest and a serious purpose. All of this has concrete meaning for your children.

The potential of the heating system in a discussion has led so far to the physical sciences and pollution of the environment. The discussion could just as easily lead to social studies. For example, one could start the questioning by asking why people heat their schools, homes, office buildings, and other places. Obviously, to keep warm. Can animals do as many things to keep warm and protected from the weather as man? Ask for a long list of comparisons between man and animal in terms of protection against weather, obtaining food, storage and protection of food supplies, and the building of structures or safe dwelling places. It turns out that man is the most adaptable of all animals, and for this reason man alone, of all the animals, is spread over the earth. Other animals are limited by weather conditions, food supplies, climate, and other factors, to particular environments. What gives man this power to adapt the environment to his needs? His intelligence? Technology? What is technology? Is it totally good? Can we harm ourselves with technology?

As for geography, where do the fuels—coal, gas, and oil—come from? The United States? Which states? How are they obtained? From outside the U.S.A.? Where?

This is using the environment as a learning experience. Why not take each of the following and use your imagination to see how it can lead off into different lines of investigations and projects for the children in your class? Keep in mind your grade level, your pupils, and your classroom. What about the lighting fixtures in your room—where can they lead? The windows? The shades? The desks? The floor? The chalkboard? The paint? The color of the paint? The school building itself—its plan? The corridors? The fire extinguishers? The fire-alarm boxes? The school bells? Paper baskets and waste? Paper and litter thrown around the school? The schoolyard? Stores in the neighborhood? A police station? A firehouse? Any trees or plants in the neighborhood? Should there be? How can one start and maintain some plants appropriate for inside a home? For a windowsill flower box?

Indoors leads outdoors. Out-of-doors there are numerous environments children and teachers can explore as "living" learning experiences. Some of these environments are: the schoolyard itself, the neighborhood of the school, a construction site, stores in the neighborhood, a vacant lot, a nearby park, and a zoological or botanical garden.

Objections most commonly given to such outdoor activities are the following: (1) The principal is against taking the children outside; (2) You need a bus for a trip. In our school it is almost impossible, or it is impossible, to obtain the services of a school bus; (3) I cannot answer most of the questions the children ask if I take them outside; (4) The children are not learning the required lessons; and (5) The parents of the children will think we just recreate and don't really stay with teaching in the classroom. A final reason which is less likely to be mentioned is the inertia of the teacher, and perhaps this is a greater obstacle than all the others.

If some of the parents of the children in your class make these outdoor trips with you, perhaps the principal will feel that the children have sufficient protection. Furthermore, this brings the parents directly into the experience. They not only participate in the learning process, but they realize the importance of the learning that takes place on such trips. The parents may also help you to persuade the principal to allow these out-of-door studies.

The bus problem is a real problem, but for many outdoor environmental experiences, no bus is necessary. There are many environments to explore within walking distances. With enough adults to insure the safety of the children, you will not need a bus for these short trips. (Later we will treat in detail how to prepare your pupils and the parents or paraprofessionals who participate as to what they might look for.) To have these outings, the teacher must first scout the environment and note some interesting things to get the children and the parents *really* looking and questioning its features. There should also be a follow-up on the experience when the children return to the classroom.

We cannot stress enough that the purpose of the trip outdoors is not to have the teacher answer questions the children raise. It is to stimulate interest and questions the children will pursue back in the classroom, singly or in groups. The outdoor experience should not be a gawking expedition. It should be unstructured in the sense that the child is out to observe, be aware, and question whatever interests him. It is structured in the sense that the teacher has given the children a focus on the kinds of things they can experience, and what the children actually find interesting will become the turn-on agents for continuing classroom learning. The research, writing, drawing, painting, storytelling, social studies, and scientific experiments that result from the outdoor experience become genuine educational experiences. The objection that children do not learn out-of-doors or that the teacher is taking a rest from teaching will not arise if this follow-up occurs. The whole purpose of exploring the out-of-doors environment is to make the children sensitively aware of these environments and to arouse their interest and curiosity. From such experiences comes the fundamental "Why?" even in the minds of very young children, and this is the beginning of learning. Once the question is asked, a problem is posed. Seeking an answer to the problem and testing one's answers is the learning process itself.

Some people feel that this is not genuine learning, but they have missed the whole point of education. What is learned in an interesting and natural setting is learned more rapidly and more deeply, and certainly these outings and follow-up investigations will be more impressive learning experiences than following an exact daily lesson plan. Furthermore, a skillful teacher with one eye on the curriculum and one eye on the children's interests can serve both of these masters. The teacher should go over curriculum requirements and carefully note the fundamental elements of the curriculum. Then by suggestive questions, or by trips planned, or by materials introduced into the classroom, the curriculum can be adequately served. We have demonstrated this at our workshops.

Of all the objections posed to out-of-doors learning experiences, the most universal, although hardly the most cogent, is teacher inertia. Many teachers just do not like all the effort involved. Some teachers heatedly ask, "Scout the place first? Make notes on interesting observations? Get the children's interest aroused? Prepare them for the out-of-doors activity? Supervise the trip? Listen to all of their questions? Control them? Follow up on their interests in the classroom?" After considering all of these things, they decide to stay in the classroom, with one lesson after the other, because it's easier in the long run.

But is it? Why are so many pupils inattentive or bored? Why do we teachers find ourselves going stale from what we are teaching? Why do we feel that teaching is a chore? Why isn't it exciting? Why aren't the children more excited about learning?

We need to be more trusting to try this different approach. Trust your children to learn gradually how to behave better on those trips by making *more* trips with them. How else can they learn? Trust your children's faith in you, even when you admit you don't know the names of trees and can't explain the local sewage system. Trust your children to learn more, even independently of you, while on the trips and back in the classroom.

We have placed no emphasis in this chapter on teachers taking their classes on trips to institutions where professional personnel at that institution take over and take the children on a tour. In this arrangement, the teacher becomes simply the one in charge of the class but not directly involved in the teaching. We have no objections to this type of trip, and they can be very helpful. We want to make it clear, however, that the environmental trips we are speaking of should be a much more frequent experience, and one that ties in the various environments with the child's learning experiences. Since the teacher is fully in charge of the activities on the environmental trips we recommend, he is able to tie them in with classroom work in a very productive way. As a matter of fact, our environmental trips render the teacher much more effective when he takes his class on a conducted tour. Having learned from many experiences with his own outings, he knows how to prepare his class for a formal tour and how to get the most learning out of the tour when the children return to the classroom. All environments, indoors or outdoors, can and should be turned into genuine learning experiences. Those teachers who have not done this to any large extent perhaps want to know how to do it. Just as things within the classroom can be used as turn-on agents, so things outside the classroom can be used as turn-on agents. Just as things that stimulate in the classroom lead outdoors, so things that stimulate children outdoors can lead indoors. Let us see more concretely how this can be done.

We can define the out-of-doors activity as any activity that takes place outside of the physical structure of the school building. Classes or small group activities that use the out-of-doors are usually one of two kinds: either the outdoor environment is used as a turn-on agent for further investigations, or an activity presently being pursued in the classroom necessitates going outdoors for further investigation and development. In the first instance, a class may have taken a neighborhood walk and brought back collections of objects found in a vacant lot, for example. In the second instance, a group of children go out to test in the March wind the kites they have constructed. No matter how the outdoor environment is used, there should always be concomitant classroom activity before, during, and after the outdoor excursions, as was suggested earlier. It is important that the child learn to use both the indoor and outdoor environment naturally in the development of a project. In this way, activities conducted primarily indoors are actively relevant to the world outside, and conversely, the out-of-doors has a definite place within the confines of the classroom.

For example, a fourth-grade class has been working for some weeks with a small group of animals. In researching the origins of the animals, they have frequently come upon the word *predator*, which they looked up in the dictionary and defined. They have also discovered what the animals eat and what the optimum conditions for their survival are. As they share their discoveries in a total class experience, it is a good opportunity for the teacher to introduce the food chain, the interdependence of living organisms, and the balance of nature. She might start with a simple classroom game called "Who Needs Who?" This game can be played in many ways on many levels. A simple way is to draw a series of pictures or sketches on a single sheet of paper. One grouping might be the sun, some grass, a pig, a lion, a zebra, some water, a boy, bacon, bacteria, some soil, a tree, and a bumblebee. Ask the children to draw a line from each picture to the other pictures that it needs to survive. Another way to play the game is to put each picture on an individual card and pin a card to each child. Provide the children with lengths of string so that they can connect to the things they need. Take away the soil and see how many other things we have to do without; take away man and see what happens. Let some of the children discuss their favorite foods and find out what is necessary to provide these foods. After a series of classroom activities designed to illustrate the interdependence of all living things the group is then ready to visit a natural site outdoors and investigate a small area for evidences of the food chain. What do the birds eat? What does the tree need? Who needs the earthworm? Who needs the bee? Samples of soil, leaves, and insects may be brought back to the classroom for further investigation. The class may decide to set up an ant farm or an earthworm farm, or to embark on a bird-feeding project, or to do some planting. Some children may do a mural illustrating the food chain for the bulletin board, while others might be inspired to write poetry or imaginative stories: "What If the Sun Decided Not to Shine," or "A Day in the Life of a Busy Worker Ant."

A fifth-grade class is compiling a booklet about species of animals that have been wiped out by man. Their visit outdoors might be to photograph or sketch an urban area, and then to investigate and reconstruct the area before the tall buildings and concrete sidewalks appeared. What forms of natural life have survived in the area? What species had to find new homes? How does a species become extinct? Why is it important that we preserve all species of life?

A group of third-graders becomes interested in the questions "Where do city children play?" and "What would be your ideal playground?" First they let their imaginations run wild and construct models of ideal playgrounds using cardboard bases and bits and pieces of wood, metal, spools, buttons, and construction paper. They then take a walk around the neighborhood to find likely sites for playgrounds. They measure the sites with trundle wheels and record the measurements. Their next outdoor visit is to an existing playground. They decide what features they like and what could be improved. They also measure to see how much room they need for a single swing or a single slide. They come back to the classroom with a more realistic picture of how many units they could put into a small area, and their second models are much more practicable. They write letters to the Department of Parks giving some of their ideas and suggestions.

A second-grade class takes a walk around the neighborhood with two inexpensive cameras, each loaded with a roll of film that will take twelve pictures. Before embarking upon the walk, they discussed two words, *beautiful* and *ugly,* which are purposely extreme words. As they walk and observe, they direct the two picture-takers to snap what they consider to be the most beautiful and the ugliest things in their school neighborhood. Some of the "beautiful" pictures turn out to be a fruit store window, a tree, a well-kept yard, and a newly painted fire-alarm box. The "ugly" pictures are piles of garbage, an abandoned, gutted frame house, a stripped car, and a defaced wall. When the pictures are developed, the children have a basis for many classroom activities aimed at improving their immediate neighborhood. The pictures are used to set up a bulletin board in the hall to ask for aid from other classes. The children then work at making their room more beautiful, and they are inspired to plan pictures that could cover the obscenities on the defaced wall. They write letters to the fruit-store owner describing how much they like his colorful display.

In the New York City schools, excursions outside the classroom are too few and too far between. The trips are usually connected with social studies and involve a trip to a museum or to a "place of interest." Many times, as we mentioned earlier, the trip is taken over by "experts" at the place, and the teacher sometimes is not involved in the educational ex-perience itself. Our attitude, however, is that taking the children *outside* the classroom to learn should be as normal, natural, and almost or just as frequent as bringing the children *into* the classroom to learn. Each trip need not be a big production; it need not involve the entire class. A few children can go outside with an aide to take rubbings from the bark of the tree in front of the school, or to count the number of cars that pass in a fifteen-minute period. We create an artificial environment by surround-ing all school learning by four walls.

Just as the child needs to learn that the outdoor environment is also an educational environment, so too must he be aware that man is de-stroying his environment. On the first Earth Day, April 22, 1970, teachers began asking for curriculum materials suitable for lower-grade classes, for upper-grade classes, and for adults. These materials were almost non-existent. Many groups have produced worthwhile materials in a little less than a year, such as the Audubon Society and the National Conservation

Association. These materials usually start by identifying the child and placing him in his immediate environment. Gradually other organisms are discussed, aiming at the concept of the interdependence of all living things. These materials are all helpful, but much more than these is needed.

We are convinced that environmental education is education for survival, and we must immediately begin to teach our children the ecological facts of life; otherwise, we may not be around long enough to worry about other educational issues. Our planet may very well become uninhabitable before satisfactory environmental curricula for all grades are developed and implemented to meet the standards of various Boards of Education and Community School Boards.

How is it possible to make water pollution vital to a seven year old? How do we communicate the urgent need for a change of attitude and for positive action? A teacher in front of a classroom "teaching" water pollution is not the answer.

If the child is to become aware of his environment; if he is to see himself as an individual acted upon by the environment, and in turn, acting upon the environment; if the child is to realize his own potential as an agent of change, then a different kind of classroom is necessary. The child becomes aware of his relation to the environment through experimentation with the many materials of the environment. The classroom setup must allow for the development of vital skills: to observe, to question, to explore, to be aware of problems, to plan, to cope with unsatisfactory results, and to try alternate solutions. A child who has had the responsibility for planning, setting up, and maintaining an aquarium in the classroom is better equipped to understand the problems of water pollution in terms of his own experiences.

In order for the student to understand today's environmental problems—air pollution, water pollution, waste pollution, and noise pollution—he must first understand the interrelationship of things, and especially of himself and nature. Education should be presented not as a set of separate subjects, but as an integrated approach to everyday living.

A small group of children want to keep a gerbil in the classroom. They must provide the animal with a home, a proper diet, and proper conditions for his survival. This one activity involves building a cage, measuring, using tools, following directions, reading, and raising money for food. The classroom experience is not fragmented into math, science, reading, and arts and crafts; rather, the integrated emphasis is upon how to solve the problem of maintaining a gerbil. The child who perceives a problem and works it through to a solution learns to value himself and to value his place in the total scheme of things. Any degradation of the environment, either in the classroom or outdoors in nature, then becomes a degradation of himself.

SELECTED READINGS

Books

BATES, MARSTON. *Man in Nature.* 2d ed. Englewood Cliffs, N.J.: Prentice-Hall, 1964.

DUBOS, RENÉ. *So Human an Animal.* New York: Scribner, 1968.

Fortune magazine editors. *The Environment: A National Mission for the Seventies.* New York: Harper & Row, 1970.

GOLDBERG, LAZER. *Children and Science.* New York: Scribner, 1970.

Provincial Committee on Aims and Objectives of Education in the Schools of Ontario. *Living and Learning.* Ontario Department of Education, 1968.

SPENCER, MARGARET. *Discovery and Experience.* London: The British Broadcasting Corporation, 1965.

Articles

These articles treat the environment topic more from the point of view emphasized in this book:

AMES, EDWARD A. "Schools and the Environment." *The Journal of Environmental Education* 2, no. 3 (Spring 1971): 1–3.

COSSA, MARIO. "Bringing 'Life' to the Classroom." *Elementary School Science Association News Letter* 10, no. 2 (Spring 1971).

HAWKINS, DAVID. "I-Thou-It." *Mathematics Teaching* (Association of Teachers of Mathematics) no. 46 (Spring 1969). (Available from Early Childhood Education Study, 55 Chapel St., Newton, Mass. 02160.)

KERLIN, SARAH M. "Rocks, Rivers, and City Children," *Childhood Education.* Washington, D.C.: (Association for Childhood Education International, January 1971).

"How to" for Teachers

COCKCROFT, W. H. *Your Child and Mathematics.* New York: John Wiley, 1968.

CRANE, JOHN, and CRANE, DIANE. *Scrap Craft.* Dansville, New York: Owen, 1963.

D'AMATO, JANET, and D'AMATO, ALEX. *Cardboard Carpentry.* Katonah, New York: Lion Press, 1966.

National Audubon Society. *A Place to Live.* Workbook and teacher's manual. New York: National Audubon Society, 1968.

———. *Audubon Ecology Study Program. Audubon Bird Study Program. Audubon Tree Study Program. Audubon Plant Study Program. Audubon Mammal Study Program.* Nature Studies Program booklets. New York: National Audubon Society, 1965–.

The Nuffield Foundation. *Autumn to Winter. Mammals in the Classroom.*

Science and History. Teachers' background booklets. London: William Collins, 1968.

——. *I Do and I Understand* (1967). *Pictorial Representation* (1967). *Beginnings.* (1968). *Computation and Structure,* 2 vols. (1968). *Shape and Size,* 2 vols. (1968). *Graphs Leading to Algebra* (1969). Nuffield Mathematics Project booklets. New York: John Wiley.

Ross, Laura. *Puppet Shows.* New York: Lothrop, Lee & Shepard, 1970.

Ruchlis, Hy. *Science Projects: Mirrors.* New York: Book-Lab, 1968.

Tannenbaum, E.; Tannenbaum, B.; Stillman, N.; Stillman, S. *Experiences in Science.* Elementary School workbook and teacher's manual. McGraw-Hill, 1968.

Books for Children

The following is a sample of types of books for grades 1, 2, and 3 that could be kept in the classroom to stimulate children's interests.

Black, Irma S. *Flipper: A Sea-Lion.* New York: Young Readers Press, 1967.

Larrick, Nancy. *Rain, Hail, Sleet, and Snow.* New York Scholastic Book Services, 1965.

Tresselt, Alvin. *The Beaver Pond.* New York: Lothrop, Lee & Shepard, 1970.

Udry, Janice May. *A Tree is Nice.* New York: Harper & Brothers, 1956.

Voight, Virginia Francis. *Lions in the Barn.* New York: Young Readers Press, 1966.

Young, Miriam. *Slow as a Snail, Quick as a Bird.* New York: Lothrop, Lee & Shepard, 1970.

The following is a sample of books for grades 4, 5, and 6.

Arnov, Boris. *Bally, the Blue Whale.* New York: Young Readers Press, 1966.

Chapman, Frank L. *Salt Marsh, Sound, and Sea Beach.* Regional Marine Science Project of the Carteret County, North Carolina, Public Schools, 1970.

Church, Robert J. *Turtles.* Jersey City, N.J.: T. F. H. Publications, 1963.

Dodd, Ed. *Mark Trail's Book of Animals.* New York: Scholastic Book Services, 1968.

Guillot, Rene. *The King of the Cats.* New York: Young Readers Press, 1966.

Hinkle, Thomas C. *Tan, a Wild Dog.* New York: Young Readers Press, 1969.

Matthews, William H. III. *The Story of Volcanoes and Earthquakes.* New York: Harvey House, 1969.

Rosenfeld, Sam. *The Magic of Electricity.* New York: Young Readers Press, 1967.

Schneider, Herman, and Schneider, Nina. *Let's Find out about Heat, Weather, and Air.* New York: Scholastic Book Services, 1969.

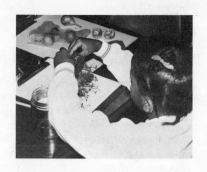

6 Learning to Live and to Share

THE SOCIAL ENVIRONMENT

The role of the school in developing social attitudes of elementary school children came up for discussion at a workshop we were recently conducting. One teacher, a woman who had taught in the New York City Public Schools for more than ten years, expressed satisfaction at the fact that the children were given some time to play in the schoolyard. "It gives them time to socialize and get to know one another," she said. "Furthermore, if the child was born into a foreign-language-speaking family and has to learn to speak English, it gives that child a chance to learn English from peers during this play period."

The sincerity of this woman was obvious. What was disturbing was the fact that she assumed the classroom itself was not the proper place for the children to develop helpful social attitudes. "Of course," she conceded, "children do learn *some* social attitudes in the classroom. The classroom helps them to learn discipline and how to behave in such a group. Then too, during the social studies period we discuss in class topics such as the differences in appearance, language and customs of different ethnic groups, the harmful effects of discrimination based on religious, economic, or ethnic grounds, and so forth." In reply to this teacher we said, "The main difference between your position and ours is that we are convinced the classroom is the place where the children should not only talk about social attitudes for part of the day, but where they should live helpful social attitudes during the entire school day as much as possible. The classroom should also be a place where children learn internal self-discipline, instead of merely following regimented patterns of external behavior demanded by the principal and the teacher."

There lies the heart of the issue. We do not question for a moment the value of class discussions on social issues. They are essential. Nor do we doubt the need for standard, purposive classroom procedures. Without these, order cannot exist. Chaos reigns where there is no order, and chaos is hardly conducive to a successful learning process.

The real question that needs answering is this: Is my classroom a continuing, *living experience* of healthy social attitudes for me and the children? If it is, then my classroom is a teaching agent of helpful social attitudes; it is an appropriate social environment. If the answer is no, it can be changed.

The social environment is dependent upon the physical, psychological, and instructional environments. Without the proper psychological environment, it is not possible to have children living helpful social attitudes in a classroom. The physical and instructional environments will reflect a proper psychological and social environment. However, let us focus more singly upon the social environment.

What are the salient features of a classroom social environment that encourage healthy social attitudes in the classroom? At the top of the list is a living conviction that each of the pupils in class is first and foremost a human person, a unique individual different from all other children. This was also the cardinal requirement for a healthy psychological environment, but we are stressing it in a different light now. The teacher and the classroom environment must encourage the child to participate fully as a member of the social group called his class. Admittedly there is a tension between social membership and individuality. However, one cannot be sacrificed for the sake of the other without hurting the child. The objective is to help the child to retain his personal integrity while participating as a member of a group. Socialization that submerges the child into the class and robs him of his uniqueness is to be discouraged. Rather, each child's individuality must be stressed *within* a healthy social environment.

The teacher must realize that every child has the right to become in his lifetime a self-directing, autonomous, and psychologically healthy person who assumes his proper responsibilities. This is an inherent right. This right is held sacred by people who value the dignity of the human person and who wish to preserve an open and free society.

The school child must enjoy an environment wherein he can develop an inner self, a set of values and goals, and a style of thinking and living that are his own—literally, *his* own. This does not deny or minimize the need the child has to be helped, guided, and influenced by beneficent resources. The younger the child is, the more dependent he is on such resources. Parents are the primary and most obvious source of help and influence. But as the child grows, he should be given the opportunities to learn to shape himself and his destiny. This learning process must take place in the classroom as well as in the home. What makes this learning process a difficult one is that a constant balance must be sought if the child is to preserve his individuality and develop healthy relationships with others.

One must not be sacrificed on the spurious grounds that it is necessary in order to develop the other. When the proper social environment exists, the individuality of the child will be given optimum opportunities for development within a context of sharing with others. Any other approach would be detrimental to the child's development as an individual. Sharing and communicating with others, relating emotionally to them, enjoying their friendship and love, experiencing their joys and heartaches, and working toward a given goal with others are essential elements of being human. This is what we mean by social. Learning, which only is an aspect of living, is social in this sense.

Of course, learning is also a private affair in the sense that the act of learning itself takes place within us. Yet the social aspect is important in a great deal of human learning. In a basic but limited sense, the foetus has been involved in the life of the mother and has had experiences that are recognized as "learning" experiences from the moment of conception up to the moment of birth. However, the learning experiences are more obvious in the child after birth. Think of the learning processes that occur as a result of the interaction between the baby and members of the social group, especially the mother, into which the child was born. The suckling process, for example, though itself a felt need, quickly develops attendant learning processes, as any mother readily recognizes.

The ongoing interplay between the child, the family, and his social group, is a continuing series of learning processes. A language must be learned. (How amazing it is that in two years the infant has a fundamental grasp on the language spoken by the family or some other immediate social group!) The child must learn to eat properly. He must be toilet trained. Our young learner not only succeeds in these learning tasks, he also explores spontaneously the strange world of people and things about him. The social aspect of the learning process is continuous. It has a pervasive influence on the learner for the rest of his life.

Teachers should capitalize on this social aspect of learning. The child learns easily from the group about him. Child psychologists have pointed out that the learning process is most rapid in the earlier years. Let us consider how this natural and spontaneous process takes place in the mind of the learner in order to know what the proper social environment in the classroom should be, if the child is to learn most effectively.

We used the word *mind*. (Should you prefer, substitute *brain, intellect, thinking function,* or whatever.) In one sense, learning is a subjective process. It takes place within the mind of the subject, the learner. We say that "I" learn. Ultimately no one else can learn for me. Others can stimulate me to learn, they can "teach" me, they can "feed" my interest to learn, but even the most solicitous and overprotective mother cannot "learn" for her child, although some try to do so. Sometimes anxious teachers, too, behave as though they could learn for their pupils.

No one can learn for another. So the most important thing for any child is to *grow as a learner*. Every human being has an innate curiosity, a need or tendency to know. It is as "natural" as eating or sleeping. The baby's senses are all "alive" from the moment of birth, contacting the world about him, receiving sights, sounds, smells, sensations of heat or cold, well-being or non-well-being, and so on. As the child learns to talk, the child asks interminable questions. The child wants to know and wants to learn to cope with things.

The child is a natural learner. As the title of a recent book has it, "Learning is Child's Play!" The child learns while "playing" and plays while "learning." There are no artificial distinctions between the one activity and the other. As a matter of fact, all of the very young child's learning is informal, and the amount they learn in this way is indeed very impressive.

Why should we not capitalize more on this basic fact and help the child to learn better how to learn? This does not mean to shift the learning process from the child to the adult, as is so frequently done, but to focus on the child's learning process and to go along with it. This means following the child's interest as long as it is not destructive. It means providing the child with an environment that allows him to learn most effectively at his present level of development. This means that the adult, whether teacher or parent, must learn to diagnose what the child is capable of grasping at any point in time. The teacher or parent must be patient and must refrain from attempting to force learning into the child's head. The child must be allowed sufficient time to explore, question, play with, wonder about, hear about, read about, experiment with, and come to conclusions before he can in any real sense learn something. If the child does not learn it even then, he must be allowed more time to do so in an unpressured manner. Pressure and anxiety are not helpful in these cases.

Honestly, what kind of peculiar compulsion do we adults experience in these circumstances? Is it not to have the child learn *now?* Or if not right now, at least in the immediate future? Why? Sometimes on the spurious theory that repetition of itself will surely get any child to learn now whatever he is supposed to learn. But isn't that absurd, when we analyze it? If a child is unable at a given stage of development to grasp a particular concept, mathematical principle, or formula, or to read "according to grade level," it may simply be because the mind of the child is not ready at that time. If this is the case, the child must be given the opportunity to gain more experience, to experiment more, to grow intellectually and emotionally before he will be able to grasp that particular concept or mathematical principle, or to read according to prescribed expectations.

Brute repetition will not get him to learn it now. Furthermore, no other coercive form of teaching will succeed either. On the contrary, if the child is given full opportunity to grow as his needs arise naturally, he will in time grasp the concept in question or come up to an expected norm of reading.

(I hope that no one will interpret the previous passages to mean that we are speaking of *every* child, even those suffering from brain damage, serious retardation difficulties, deep-seated psychoses, or similar major handicaps. These children need expert diagnosis and professional care. No general method of education can overcome such problems by itself. But we do wish to include those children who all too frequently are shunted aside as slow learners, low achievers, slow readers, and the like. These children feel defeated or humiliated in a classroom that does not allow for individual rates of growth. These same children feel at home in a classroom that puts the premium on what each child accomplishes within his limits, and not on standardized objective performance tests.)

Not a few parents, and in our experience, an unexpectedly large number of educators who should know better, become apprehensive when children in a given class do not perform in a standard way within what they deem to be tolerable variations. They fear that unless they demand standards of their pupils, the pupils will cease to learn properly. There are two basic assumptions underlying their position: Children possess neither the willingness nor discipline to learn what they must learn "to succeed in life"; and education of the young is best attained when the matter to be learned is clearly set out in a curriculum by experienced educators, and pupils are required in terms of objective performance tests to meet certain established standards.

Among professional psychologists, the behaviorists have promoted this point of view as a genuinely "scientific" one. That the behaviorist method has valid applications and has proven successful for specific purposes is substantiated beyond question. If, for example, one wishes to set precisely defined type of behavior as a goal for human endeavor, then a conditioning process can be used, and the results can be tested in terms of an objective performance test. But our basic objection to applying the behaviorist method generally to education, and particularly to elementary education, is that it places far too much attention and stress on results judged by objective performance tests rather than the individual growth and learning style of the child. We think that the child's individual formation is more important in the long run than his being conditioned to perform specific tasks in the present. In our opinion, as long as the major emphasis is on the child's individual learning process, techniques developed by the behaviorists can be used to great advantage. However, they are fundamentally conditioning processes, and they do look for quantitatively measurable results.

The vast weight of contemporary findings in developmental psychology point not to uniformity of development and performance in children, but to great differences in development and performance by children of the same chronological ages. It also points to the necessity of considering the variety of needs, talents, and the uniqueness of each child, if one is to help the child grow as a learner. In line with these findings, we maintain that the proper purpose of education is not to train the young in uniform fashion to attain objectives predetermined as essential. Anyone who has studied the history of education with an analytical mind knows that each culture establishes different objectives of education, and succeeding generations of a culture change the objectives to reflect the felt needs and competing value systems. It has been pointed out that the average man in our contemporary society will have to change his marketable skills two to three times to meet the changes in technological development, methods of production, and the demand for new skills. According to reliable predictions, this trend will increase rather than decrease. The younger generations must be ready for this. They must be prepared for their future society, and their education must encourage self-development in the learning process itself, a flexibility in learning diverse skills, and an openness to new ideas and new methods. Any contemporary educational practice that locks the learner tightly into set bodies of knowledge will sooner or later leave that person with knowledge that is outdated and unreliable, and skills that are no longer marketable.

We are not saying that content is unimportant. Content is important, but in a relative sense. It is more important for the child to learn where to find and how to use content than it is for the child to memorize, or "learn" if you will, definite content, as if the content is the sole important goal. The most important goal is for the child to grow as a learner, and that means *how* to analyze and solve problems; where to go to find needed information; how to use reliable information to solve problems and to attain goals; how to evaluate critically what he learns from himself and others; how to assess the strong points and the limitations of the scientific method, how to evaluate and use his inventive and creative powers; and how to learn from others who are more qualified in a given area. These are some of the elements of the learning process that the child should acquire as he develops.

It is important for the child to learn the difference between poor quality and good work. The question is how? We believe it is best done not by proposing a universal standard for the entire class to meet, but by having the child evaluate his own work with the teacher's assistance. With the proper suggestions, the teacher can at times offer a challenge within the reach of that particular student to do a better job. In this manner, no child feels that he is defeated from the start by being required to emulate a standard that at this point in time (and what else really exists for the child) he knows he cannot reach. Growth in quality is like growth in anything else. One must take one step at a time according to one's own capabilities. By taking this attitude in class, the teacher sets up a social environment wherein each person (children and teacher) in the room is respected as an individual for his or her own sake.

The most important norm here is self-development, not the meeting of "objective standards." Individual differences are accepted as perfectly natural. The atmosphere in this type of classroom is acceptance of the other *as other* in a warm spirit of cooperative venture. All are learning together, teacher and children alike. Just as the teacher endeavors not to dominate, but to help each child or group of children, so each child is encouraged to help the other. The ability to relate well to others and to work cooperatively with others is developed as a normal classroom attitude, since it is the attitude we would want the children to have in and out of the classroom.

The apparent dispute about schools of psychology (behaviorism versus developmental psychology) boils down to a choice between two radical value judgments about the way one looks upon a child. Do you want to view a school child as a competitor who must be measured against other competitors, who develops a self-image of himself as successful or unsuccessful in relation to standards and his classmates? If so, then objective performance tests, age-reading-levels, and other "statistically objective" norms are the proper way to judge the performance of elementary school children. Children are placed in tight categories of age, grade level, or whatever, and their precise performance in a specified assignment is measured. One can then tell whether a child is up to a standard derived from peer performance. Then one knows how this child fits into his social group and into society in general.

On the other hand, if you view the child as a unique individual who should be allowed to grow and mature according to his own physiological and psychological abilities, then it is apparent that his growth cannot be adequately compared with anyone else's. You envision the child as fitting into society not with a worth determined by his comparative achievement, but in accord with a socialization process that accepts him as he is and for what he can contribute. You should have the patience to work in and through his own unique stages of development.

We are not rejecting any and all examinations that seek to establish some standards of performance. We simply think that the field of testing has been preempted by the behaviorists, and that far greater emphasis should be centered in the elementary schools on the developmental aspects of the individual child. At present, teaching in the elementary schools is generally aimed at having the children perform well on objective performance tests rather than at genuine development of the individual child. We can reverse this trend only if the physical, psychological, and instructional environments of the classroom make it possible. When children are permitted to work on projects singly or in groups, when children are permitted to speak to others as they move about the classroom on their projects, when they share the results of their individual and group accomplishments, when they help plan their future work together, when they have meetings to discuss the disciplinary problems that arise and how to solve them, when they live a *real* life of interaction with other human beings in a meaningful way, they create a social environment that becomes a teaching agent itself.

In such a social environment, children realize early in life that human beings can learn a great deal from one another, if each is willing to share. This is in contrast with the classroom situation where children sit in rows, for the most part silent, while the teacher explains the lesson or has them do an assignment. The children there have little opportunity to learn from one another.

In the method we propose, the children learn from many people each day. They learn from the teacher, but they also learn a great deal from one another. We have observed this in various classrooms taught by teachers in his program. We have witnessed it in most dramatic form in nongraded summer programs conducted at Wave Hill for public school children. Two children who seemed most unlikely to work together were two boys we shall call José and Mohandas. José's parents had come from Puerto Rico, did not speak English well, and were poor. The neighborhood in which they lived was very run-down. José would have been described by some teachers as "culturally deprived" and a "low achiever." By contrast, Mohandas would have been considered very alert, very intelligent, and very well-informed, especially for a boy eight years old. His father was a professor of physics and his mother was equally well-educated. What had these two youngsters in common? Apparently nothing. One day, however, Mohandas was experimenting with some science materials. José stood watching, fascinated. Mohandas very spontaneously started to explain to José what he was doing. In no time at all both were working away assiduously on the experiment. José was learning a

great deal of science from Mohandas. Was this to be all a one-way learning process, we wondered as we watched them?

For a time, yes, Mohandas was the leader. But as José caught on and
became more and more interested, he began to pose questions to Mohandas that showed insight and gave a real challenge to Mohandas. Then
they decided to do a project together. Now new skills entered, and José
had an artistic flair and innate skill that came to the fore. He then took
the lead and Mohandas was mainly the learner. So it went. One child's
strength helped develop the other child as the days went by.

We mention this incident for another reason. It has been cogently
argued in scholarly articles, and persuasive evidence has been presented
to support the hypothesis that heterogeneous grouping, while beneficial
for low achievers, slow learners, and even for average pupils, is detrimental to the highly gifted child. The latter, it is said, spends too much
time teaching the ones slower than he. He does not receive the high
degree of challenge he needs from children not as gifted as he. The highly
gifted child, the argument continues, needs other highly gifted children
and a very superior teacher to continuously offer him serious challenges.
Only thus can he achieve *his* greatest potential.

The argument on paper is quite compelling. In some circumstances,
moreover, it is undoubtedly true that the highly gifted child could be
held back in his own development by spending his time serving the needs
of the less gifted. But the situation need not be this way. In the first
place, if a teacher has been properly trained to conduct an open classroom with heterogeneous grouping, he knows that no child should be
allowed to occupy, willingly or unwillingly, the position of teacher-for-
the-slower children. It is true that some teachers, even with a homogene-
ously composed class, use brighter students to teach the slowest. While at
times this can be constructive for both, it can also be harmful to the
brighter. Obviously it depends on whether the teacher is looking to
help each child or looking to ease his burdens. A gifted child can receive
very demanding challenges from other children in a classroom. When he
is not being so challenged and stimulated, the teacher must help the
highly gifted child to select an area of experimentation, research, writing,
or whatever, that will fully challenge him. It has been our experience
that when such care is taken the highly gifted child does reach his maximum potential.

There is, however, a further point to be made. Highly gifted children
in severe competition with one another can rapidly advance intellectually. They can also neglect the social and human side of life to such an
extent that they become emotional cripples with little understanding of
people less gifted than themselves and unable to deal with the heterogeneous groupings of people found in everyday life. We think that it is

extremely important, especially for the highly gifted child, to develop as fully emotionally and socially as he does intellectually.

We are not watering down the right of the highly gifted child to develop his full potential intellectually as well as emotionally and socially. Precisely because teachers must guard this right, we recommend a style of teaching that establishes a social environment in the classroom that fosters opportunities for each individual to pursue singly or in groups the learning experience that will help him *as an individual* to grow most effectively. This means that they can learn not only from the teacher and one another, but also from many other people. They learn from adults purposely invited into the classroom to share their expertise with the children. And there is no reason why selected adults should not on occasion be invited to present a special challenge to highly gifted children.

The children also learn from shopkeepers, construction workers, members of service companies, and similar sources in the neighborhood. They learn from the people to whom they write letters for needed information. They learn from books, too, because individual reading on topics of interest is strongly encouraged, and the opportunity for such reading is readily available. Since the teacher in this type of classroom does not pose as *the* authority, the children come to realize that a vast amount of knowledge is stored up in books to which they can go for help. The children are not made to read a textbook for the sake of improving their reading. They unwittingly improve their reading when they go to books to discover whatever they want to know or enjoy. Reading becomes a sharing of another person's thoughts, feelings, discoveries, and dreams. They learn to read better by reading more, and because they *want* to read, they do read more.

To such a child as he grows up, books on art, physics, music, biology, mathematics, chemistry, and literature are not closed mysteries as they are for so many children. They are voices of human beings who wrote down what they wanted to share with other human beings. To have our pupils catch this spirit, we have to make the classroom environment a place where learning and living is shared. They must come to realize that sharing, learning, knowledge, and living are like sharing love. You do not lose anything in the giving. Rather, you receive more by sharing your gift with others.

In the summer programs we have conducted for young children (grades 1–3), we purposely mixed the children according to ethnic, socio-economic, and educational achievement backgrounds. Though from different public schools and from different geographical areas, the children got along well from the start, as could have been predicted. In a short while they were intermingling freely and associating warmly with one another despite their individual backgrounds. Of course, disputes of the type that are normal among children did arise. These, too, were independent of individual backgrounds. These occasions were used by the teachers to have discussions with the group of children to clarify the guidelines for good social behavior. Prejudice, a popular song reminds us on radio and TV, has to be carefully taught. Good or bad social behavior is learned too. Children need to learn what is right and what is wrong, and why. But they must have the opportunity to relate to other children freely and spontaneously in order to do so. A formal classroom setting permits very little of this. An open classroom grants much greater freedom.

Of course, freedom under these conditions is not a license to do as one pleases. On the contrary, the child learns how to use freedom constructively in a social context. The implicit message the teacher gets across to the children by his own behavior and by the style of behavior he encourages in the children is that the other person is as important as I am. The teacher helps them to understand that freedom, when enjoyed properly, has limits. With freedom goes the corresponding responsibility to respect the freedom of others. This means they should acknowledge and protect the rights of others and be sensitive to their feelings. By having the children vary the other children with whom they work on projects, each child gets to associate sooner or later with all of the other children in the classroom. Thus they learn how to relate to widely different children.

In many traditional classrooms, on the other hand, the children come to know one another mainly in terms of each child's public class performance. Susan, for example, gets to be known as the best artist in the class; Richard as the mathematician. Harry is dubbed the class clown; Deborah, the worst reader. It is rare in such a class for one child to know another as a real person. This is hardly a proper environment in which to learn how to relate well to other people. It is only by allowing children to relate personally to one another in a classroom that they can live healthy social relationships in and outside the classroom.

It should be evident by now that we believe it is important for the child to develop in the classroom a strong sense of obligation as a member of society to help the social order. The reason is that the social order is the social environment in which we all live. The environment has significant effect on us. If for no other reason than the pragmatic self-serving one of our own good, we should be interested in a healthy social environment. Altruistic ethical convictions or religious beliefs about loving one's neighbor as oneself should only enforce any conviction about the necessity of our contributing to the social order to make it a better one. Why should this important part of life be omitted from the total classroom environment? It should be an intrinsic part of classroom living, and the methods we suggest in this book help to make it so.

The child is a human being with social needs. The child wishes to communicate with the teacher and the other children and to share discoveries, successes, failures, feelings, wants, doubts, and all the other human reactions. The child has a need to learn progressively the art of loving others and the art of dealing with others on a personal basis. The child needs to learn how to grow in playing, working, conversing, laughing, singing, dancing with other children. All of this should be part of social living. All of this should be part of classroom living, because classroom living should be genuine social living.

Everything that has been said in this chapter revolves around the central idea of every child's uniqueness. Each child is unique by virtue of all that makes this child to be what he is: his genetic code, his previous upbringing, his developing character traits, present background, emotional dispositions, physical well-being, and so forth. The emphasis must always be placed here.

Learning has a social element to it in the many senses we have just explored. Human beings learn much from the accumulated wisdom of countless other human beings, past and present. Furthermore, we all learn many things in the social context of home, neighborhood, social gatherings, sports, and play. But ultimately, it is the individual who learns, and the individual child can only learn in accord with his own makeup, stage of development, and ability. Every individual child must be the center of the social group that makes up the classroom. The social life—the interaction of teacher with pupils, of child with other children—must be predicated on that basis.

There are two generic ways of looking upon society. One considers the group as a whole to be the most important factor. Teachers with this view generally consider the needs of the whole class more important than the needs of the individuals who compose the class. The other way of looking upon society considers the individual the most important factor and sees the group merely as individuals joined together in cooperative venture. Teachers with this latter point of view generally consider the needs of individuals as most important, and they handle group problems only when they know that several children share, as individuals, in the common need. We prefer the latter viewpoint.

Children must grow from within and learn for themselves, as much as possible, how to learn. They should develop a good self-image and become active, self-directed, participating members of society. To the extent that this goal can be accomplished, society will be made up of dynamic individuals who form a cohesive whole. To the extent that it is not accomplished, society will be an artificial whole held together tenuously by external structures and decaying institutions.

If the responsible exercise of human freedom in any genuine sense is to survive socially and politically, we believe it can only do so with the generic type of education espoused in this book. We do not think that the goal of education should be to promote or perpetuate a single social or political system. We do think that one of the goals of education should be to prepare the young to take over the responsibility of deciding freely and intelligently which social and political structures will be most helpful for themselves and their fellow citizens. The social environment of the classroom is an important means to that end.

SELECTED READINGS

Books

ANASTASI, ANNE. *Psychological Testing*. 3d ed. New York: Macmillan, 1968.

BANDURA, A.; and WALTERS, R. *Social Learning and Personality Development*. New York: Holt, Rinehart & Winston, 1963.

BIRCH, H.; and GUSSOW, J. *Disadvantaged Children*. New York: Harcourt Brace Jovanovich, 1970.

BLOOM, BENJAMIN S., and KRATHWOHL, D. R. *Taxonomy of Educational Objectives. Handbook I: Cognitive Domain*. (1956). *Handbook II: Affective Domain* by D. Krathwohl, D. Bloom, B. Masia (1964). New York: David McKay.

COOPER, GERTRUDE E. *The Place of Play in an Infant and Junior School*. London: National Froebel Foundation, 1966. (Available from National Froebel Foundation, 2 Manchester Square, London, W.1.)

FARGO, GEORGE A.; BEHRNS, CHARLENE; and NOLEN, PATRICIA. *Behavior Modification in the Classroom*. Belmont, Calif.: Wadsworth, 1970.

FROMM, ERICH. *The Art of Loving*. New York: Bantam Books (H2563), 1963.

GARDNER, DOROTHY E. *Experiment and Tradition in Primary Schools*. London: Methuen, 1966.

JOHNSON, RONALD C.; and MEDINNUS, GENE R. *Child Psychology: Behavior and Development*. New York: John Wiley, 1965.

KIRSCHENBAUM, H.; SIMON, S.; and NAPIER, R. *Wad-ja-get?: The Grading Game in American Education*. New York: Hart, 1971.

KVARACEUS, WILLIAM C.; GIBSON, JOHN S.; PATTERSON, FRANKLIN; SEASHOLES, BRADBURY; and GRAMBS, JEAN D. *Negro Self-Concept*. New York: McGraw-Hill, 1965.

MILLER, HARRY L. *Education for the Disadvantaged*. New York: Free Press, 1962.

TORRANCE, E. P. *Guiding Creative Talent*. Englewood Cliffs, N.J.: Prentice-Hall, 1962.

WITTY, PAUL A. *The Gifted Child*. New York: D. C. Heath, 1951.

7 But Will They Be Able to Read and Write?

THE INSTRUCTIONAL ENVIRONMENT

"What about teaching the basic skills?" is a question that comes up early and frequently in every environmental workshop program. The prominence in the educational system of the metropolitan reading scores, the various objective performance tests, and the new contract accountability clause all loom large in the teachers' minds. Another frequent comment is "I am so busy teaching the basic skills that I do not have time for experimentation or play." To answer these objections, let us first examine what the basic skills are and how they are being taught at present. Second, let us evaluate the overall measure of success that teachers can claim in teaching the basic skills. The statistics are rather frightening and reveal, if examined closely, that many children leave school without acquiring the basic skills, despite the teachers' efforts. Finally, let us consider ways in which the skills can be taught more effectively.

We usually find that all teachers completely agree with us up to a certain point. We all agree that a child should learn to read fluently with comprehension, that he should learn to communicate easily both orally and by writing, and that he should acquire the basic fundamentals of arithmetic. We are in complete agreement about the importance of the child's developing the basic skills, but we disagree about the method.

We regard the basic skills as tools for learning, and we believe the child should learn and appreciate them as tools. Skills learned for their own sake are far less effective than skills learned as tools with which the child can operate more successfully in his environment. The method whereby these basic skills are learned should be part of the child's overall environment. Consider the following example from a fourth-grade class.

One of the prescribed fourth-grade writing skills is learning the correct forms for writing several kinds of letters. Sample letters appear in the English textbook and workbook. Many children in the fourth grade have had little or no opportunity to write any kind of letter in their short lifetimes, and they see none in the foreseeable future. However, being conscientious students, they promptly memorize the forms and just as promptly forget them. The teacher "covered" the curriculum material, but learning did not take place. By contrast, the group of children we spoke of in a previous chapter, who wanted to learn more about some tiles acquired from a construction site, decided to write a letter to several tile companies requesting information. They were most anxious to get the letter just right so their request would be honored. After they learned the form and wrote their letters, they filed a copy in their logs for future reference. These children also served as a resource group for other children who wanted to write for information. Similarly, the children who set up the class post office became experts in writing friendly letters and did not hesitate to share their knowledge with their classmates. By the end of the year, each child knew how to write a friendly letter and a letter in which a request is made. A fourth-grade basic skill was taught in the context of the instructional environment of this classroom.

For our purposes in this chapter, the discussion of the instructional environment focuses on the method by which the child learns the basic skills. If we consider the basic skills to be reading, writing, and arithmetic, we would have to agree that reading ranks first in the hierarchy of learning in the New York City schools. If our method of education does not motivate a child to read, improve his word-attack skills, and strengthen his comprehension of written matter, then it is not a good method for our schools. The environmental method we are proposing does motivate the child in these ways. Because of our success with recalcitrant readers, we also maintain that it does so better than formal reading instruction before the whole class. From the moment the teacher sets up his first child-centered corner of the room, reading becomes a necessity. Objects are labeled and projects are described with vocabulary relevant to the child's interests and needs. A first-grader may learn *magnet, magnetic,* and *magnetize* from labels on a discovery table before he learns *in* and *on.* But if he dictates his story about his experience with magnets to the teacher and the story is used to help him develop reading vocabulary, he will learn the little words quickly enough. Children come to school recognizing *snap, crackle, and pop* and *bubble gum* because these words are relevant to their experiences outside the classroom.

Books, magazines, posters, charts, and direction sheets are vital in a classroom set up with interest centers. First the child is attracted by the manipulative materials and he begins to play. At some point in his play, he begins to realize the value of illustrations in a book. Many times the child's curiosity is whetted by an illustration. He longs to find out more about what is illustrated, so he begins to realize the value of the printed word. The words in a book not only tell him about the materials he is using, but often they instruct him how to use the materials. The books are there not only for the child to look up answers to questions, but to give him interesting ideas to pursue. For example, an animal center stocked with live animals, models, cages, food, measuring materials, art, and recording materials might include the following books:

Bauer, Margaret J., *Animal Babies*. New York: Donahue, 1967

Dodd, Edward. *Mark Trails' Book of Animals*. New York: Scholastic Book Service, 1955

Pistorius, Anna. *What Butterfly Is It?* New York: Follett, 1955

Rood, Ronald. *Bees, Bugs, and Beetles*. New York: Scholastic Book Service, 1965

Schmidt, Karl. *Homes and Habits of Wild Animals*. New York: Donohue, 1934

Zim, Herbert S. *Alligators and Crocodiles*. New York: Scholastic Book Service, 1952

The selection of books on any subject should range from simple picture books to a more sophisticated, scientific treatment.

The children who work in this environmental education method keep daily-experience logs recording their discoveries and describing their projects. The children able to write rather easily keep their own logs and help their less facile classmates. They are constantly in need of new vocabulary to express their ever-expanding discoveries. Children who are verbally facile but read and write poorly may dictate their experiences into a tape recorder for later written recording by the teacher or by another pupil. This written recording can then serve as a reading experience for the children who have worked on the project, or for another group of children to share the project.

In the lower grades, the teacher may keep a daily-experience chart log for the entire class, recording the highlights of their discovery period. This log is useful in reorienting the children on subsequent days and also to reinforce reading experience. The experience log should consist of stories, outlines, charts, pictures, diagrams, and graphs, so that different kinds of writing and reading skills are exercised.

As in the individualized reading program reading skills are taught individually as the need arises. As the child's reach exceeds his grasp, he needs more difficult books and more complicated recording skills. Individual or small group lessons with new vocabulary introduced and skills like "getting the main idea" or "use of inflected endings" help the child to advance in reading and therefore to advance his project. The vocabulary he acquires on a given day is the vocabulary he needs to advance his interest in many different directions. The child's project is a motivating force in his selection of books. Making a puppet may lead him to simple plays and poetry or to investigate a musical instrument.

Working with materials in the environmental method increases verbalization, increases vocabulary, and strengthens the concepts underlying good reading comprehension. When children experiment with manipulative materials, there are no right or wrong answers; only observations. Children have a positive feeling of success when they build something or make something work. This feeling of success leads to a desire to share, to verbalize about a project without fear of being labeled wrong or a failure.

As the child deals with more materials, he needs more vocabulary to express himself. He is self-motivated to increase his vocabulary because of a felt need. Many of our disadvantaged children have poor reading comprehension because the printed word does not call up a clear referent. As the child works with different materials and develops a vocabulary for them, his storehouse of clear referents increases. For example, when he encounters the word *flowing* in its printed form, the concept of a "river" he has developed by pouring water over an inclined pile of gravel will give concrete meaning to the idea behind the word.

It has been our experience that this environmental method stimulates the children to do a great deal of writing and recording. Their written materials are used in displays and on bulletin boards, and are collected into bound booklets for the other children to explore and enjoy. Other children are stimulated to read about and experiment with materials. The children are continually contributing to and building up their own resource library so that the reference section of the classroom is a living, growing thing, relevant to the needs of the particular grroup of children.

In almost every kind of exploration or project there comes a time when the child needs some kind of reference material. It is incumbent upon the teacher to foresee this need and to have available pertinent maps, magazines, books, and charts. For example, if a group is working on foods and has focused on coffee beans, then a map of South America, magazine ads for different brands of coffee, recipes using coffee, and charts showing coffee consumption in the United States might be made available at that interest center. The reading and spelling vocabulary for this group for the week might include words such as coffee, dessert, instant, percolator, sugar, cream, and flavor. Ultimately the words will be shared with the entire group when the project is shared. Reading occurs as a result of self-motivated activities, and the child feels the need to improve his reading skills. This self-motivation carries over into the formal reading period that is mandatory in most schools.

One of the teachers in our workshop is in a school district that directs teachers to use "Project Read"—a total reading program, including workbooks, exercises, etc.—for a prescribed time each day. He reports that the children have been much more motivated during the formal reading period for two reasons: first, they are starting to relate the process of learning to read to working on and completing their projects; second, they know that as soon as the quiet, structured formal reading period is over, they will be able to work in a less formal, more relaxed atmosphere on their projects. Other teachers have come to us with specific requests for reading materials for a child with a history of "doing nothing" in school. A fifth-grade child, frequently truant, became interested in birds. A book about birds on a third-grade reading level, material on the human skeleton, and a vocabulary for textures all became relevant reading materials for this child's experience. The child who is achieving well at above grade level is unfettered; he is free to read and explore far beyond the bounds of the curriculum for his grade. The vocabulary and comprehension the gifted child develops is relevant to *his* interest and achievement. In this way, reading is used as a tool, and is used in a different manner by each child, but all are growing in skill.

If we examine the many reasons why people read—for information, for vicarious experience, to keep abreast of the news, to discover new ideas, to avoid danger, for pleasure, for enjoyment of poetry and literature—we find that a method of education in which a child pursues projects based on his own interests will motivate the child to read.

Mathematics is an integral part of the instructional environment of every classroom. The basic materials in every classroom should include the various measuring devices from scales to stopwatches, and many counting and computing aids from the abacus to the mini-computer. Many of the mathematics materials can be made by the children or collected from salvage materials. Duplicating geoboards and balance scales calls upon the children's ingenuity, and making them is an educational experience in itself. Various-sized jars and cans are easily collected. They can be used for a variety of purposes, from mixing paint for art work to measuring volumes. If we regard these materials as purely mathematical materials, only to be taken out during the arithmetic lesson and promptly put away, we are unnecessarily restraining the children. Some of these materials are inherently attractive and may serve as turn-on agents. Small children can work with a balance scale for hours, experimenting with the notions of "heavier," "lighter," and "equal to." Results can be recorded in pictures, ($\bigcirc$ $\bigcirc$ $\bigcirc$ $=$ $\circ\,{}^\circ_\circ\,\circ$) or words, ("Three lima beans equal five wooden beads"). Older children can use the balance scale as a model for constructing their own balances, determining proportions, cooking, scientific experiments, a discussion of equations, illustrating the concept of justice, or as the starting point of an exploration of the balance of nature. The balance is listed in the school catalog as a mathematical material, but it becomes a tool for exploration in many other areas.

Other mathematical materials are merely tools for solving everyday problems. It is necessary for the child to learn the skills necessary to use these tools effectively. A thermometer is only useful if its number line can be read and interpreted, and differences in temperature recorded. Thirty degrees has no meaning unless the child associates it with cold and knows that a twenty degree increase would be considerably warmer.

In a sixth-grade class, a group of girls who are turned on by a pile of multicolored fabrics of various textures are testing the effects of hot, cold, and warm water on the fabrics. The teacher takes a few moments to review reading the thermometer with them. When they are ready to record their conclusions, they begin by writing out all their observations. One child suggests that they save time by making a chart. When they share their chart with the rest of the class, the entire class participates in helping them graph their findings for the bulletin board. Their dictionary words for the week include *temperature, thermometer, shrink, pucker,* and *discolor.* These words are now added to their spelling lists. (In formal education, these girls had been reading on a third-grade level and were on level two in spelling.) When we returned to this class three weeks later, the girls took great pride in showing us that they could still spell their "big words." Moreover, they regarded the basic mathematical skill, the ability to read a thermometer, as a means to operate more effectively.

A geoboard with a variety of colored rubber bands is a mathematical tool that can lead to an understanding of geometric shapes, angles, area, and perimeter. It is also a useful tool in mapping and in art designing. It is a viable means of communicating with a non-English-speaking child. A little Spanish child who spoke no English used her rubber bands to make a picture of a house. With this house the teacher was able to communicate that a square has four equal sides, a rectangle has four sides not equal, and a triangle has three sides. As the child understood and learned the terms, the teacher wrote them for her, and she illustrated them from her house. Her smile of delight with the magic of the geoboard was gratifying to observe.

We use mathematics in real life situations every day of our lives when we go to the supermarket, take a pleasure ride in an automobile, and plan our day. Most of life's activities require a knowledge of time, measurement, number, and computation. Yet when we teach these skills to children, we tend to separate them from real life, and these skills become very abstract and difficult. To cope with this difficulty, teachers usually present these abstract mathematical concepts in a series of problems to which the child may or may not relate. Instead, why not start with a project or a problem chosen by the child out of his own interest or desire and teach the mathematical skills needed for that problem? Why not trust that during the course of the school year, all the children pursuing their interests will need the skills of measuring, telling time, counting, and computing?

A group of fifth-graders decided to experiment with baking. They found a recipe for a dozen cupcakes. The teacher agreed to let them bake only if they made enough cupcakes for the entire class. This required altering the recipe and adding and multiplying fractions. Since the entire class was to partake of the fruits of their labor, the group asked the entire class to participate in translating and checking the recipe. The teacher called the entire class together and "led" a lesson in adding fractions. Since they had to triple the recipe, it was necessary to change 1/4 of a cup of sugar and 2/3 of a cup of milk: $1/4 + 1/4 + 1/4 = 3/4$; $2/3 + 2/3 + 2/3 = 6/3$, which is the same as two whole cups. The cupcakes were delicious and the homework assignment, which had to do with fractions, was regarded as an interesting and challenging game.

"But what about sequence?" the traditional educator may point out. "Is the teaching of mathematics not dependent upon following a certain sequence? In this environmental method, things seem to be taught out of sequence."

Sequence, we must remember, is merely a guide. Would you teach addition of fractions to a child who does not have the vaguest notion of what a fraction is?

When a child pursues a problem in the environmental method, he supplies us with an almost perfect guideline for the sequence that is most meaningful and relevant to him. Can we ask for a better clue?

On Monday, January 5, at 1:45 P.M., Johnny, Susan, Dorothy, and Steve need to learn clock arithmetic. A small group lesson of about twenty minutes is called for with a follow-up activity and a homework assignment. At this point, clock arithmetic is not relevant to the pursuits of the remainder of the class. Some children are way beyond it and some are not ready for it. Does the instructional environment of your classroom allow twenty minutes to teach a basic skill to four children who are motivated and ripe for it?

Writing has long been considered the culmination of the language arts sequence. Extensive writing is postponed in many traditional classrooms until the reading skills are mastered. However, we find a great flow of writing from the earliest grades on, starting with captions for pictures and leading up to pages of description and explanation, when an environmental approach is used.

A sixth-grade teacher assigned a composition topic to her class, using the open-ended sentence, "I believe . . ." The children discussed possibilities and were then given a half hour to write their compositions. Sheila squirmed, made faces, chewed her pencil, and at the end of the half hour came up with the following composition:

I BELIEVE

I believe in the next 25 to 50 years we will be wearing our hair and our clothes like in the days of the 1860s.

Weeks later, after the teacher decided to change her method, Sheila was in a group that was working with Rusty the guinea pig. At 2:40 P.M. one afternoon the children completed their cleanup and started the entries in their discovery logs. Sheila produced the following in ten minutes:

Animals (Rusty sounds like a typewriter when she eats paper)
Rusty (Gini-Pig)
Her color is rust. She has approximately 20 wiskers. She bites food with her upper and lower teeth and chews it with two teeth she has on the top ridge of her mouth.
She likes to bite and nibble on the outside of things. She chews paper and eats it like it were some kind of vegetable. She likes to be held securely on her bottom paws and she squeeks when she's hungry or wants to be put down. She also talks by squeeking. Her face is like a squirrel's face and her body is like a rabbit's body. She has 2 feet in the front and four little toenails on each foot. She has 2 long hind feet with 3 long toenails on each foot.

Teachers working in the environmental method of education have reported without exception that children observe a great deal, have a great deal to share, and their discoveries ultimately lead to a large amount of writing. The writing may be done by the child himself, or it can be dictated to another child or an adult. It may be part of a class experience or it may be dictated into a tape recorder for recording at a later time. The writing takes many forms: a story about an animal, like the story about Rusty; or an imaginative story *If I were a Guinea Pig;* or data on a chart, a puzzle, a poster, or a graph.

A fourth-grade youngster, working on a weather project, became interested in the daily newspaper accounts of weather in different sections of the United States. He made daily weather maps for a week, using the symbols he had taken from a book on weather. In the course of his research he developed a sizable weather vocabulary. Wishing to share this vocabulary with the class, he developed the crossword puzzle shown on page 76.

After the children have worked in the environmental method for a period of time, they become quite adept at writing imaginative stories because they have become accustomed to having something to say. The following story was written by a third-grade boy.

If I Were a Plant

I would like to be a plant because I would not have to go to school. I would like to stand in the sun all day. I would like to give vegatables or fruits.

Here is a picture of the way I would look.

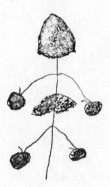

His third-grade classmate came to the following rather mature conclusions after a period of experimentation with many materials.

Science

Everything has something to do with science.. There is a world of science below you and above you. The science ways of insects are about how they do the different jobs for us and why they do it. The science ways of plants are how their seeds are blown by the wind and grow into flowers and trees. As we go higher in science, we come to rockets. The scientific ways of the astronauts are to find out things on the moon. Then we go to science above rockets, the sun and the planets and the stars. After you have learned quite a lot of science, you will see how easy it is.

Writing is important at every phase of discovery, from the simple act of writing down a number when a child is timing something to writing a play for the paper-bag puppets to perform. The writing flows easily because it is highly motivated. The skills needed to improve writing are

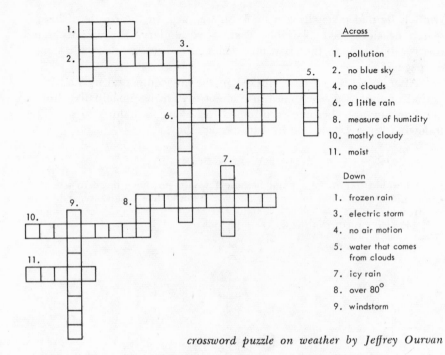

Across

1. pollution
2. no blue sky
4. no clouds
6. a little rain
8. measure of humidity
10. mostly cloudy
11. moist

Down

1. frozen rain
3. electric storm
4. no air motion
5. water that comes from clouds
7. icy rain
8. over 80°
9. windstorm

crossword puzzle on weather by Jeffrey Ourvan

gleaned from the writings themselves. From Sheila's story about Rusty, the teacher can select her spelling words, such as *whiskers* and *guinea pig*. Sheila could also use some help in paragraphing. The children who wrote the essay about science could benefit from some work on sentence structure. The writing skills taught can be tailored to the child's needs. I can think of no greater waste of time than an "English lesson" to the whole class on the use of quotation marks when only about seven children in the class actually need or are ready to learn it. No wonder we have so many discipline problems, when we teach skills that part of the class already knows and part of the class is not ready for. This wastes valuable classroom time.

For most of us, writing rarely becomes an end in itself; it is merely a means to an end. We write to communicate with another person, to register a complaint, to record an important event, or to help clarify our thinking. It should be expressed as naturally as expressing ourselves verbally. Why then do we surround classroom writing with such an aura of artificiality? The mere "selection" of a topic creates an artificial situation. In the environmental method the writing comes as naturally as speaking. It becomes important to the child because it creates a permanent record of something he has pursued with great interest. It states his own observations and conclusions. With a little help, his writing skill improves with each entry in his log. (We have discussed writing as a skill in this section. Logs will be discussed in more detail in a later chapter on recordkeeping.)

The instructional environment of the classroom not only teaches the basic skills as they become relevant to the children's needs and interests, but it also teaches the basic skills in an interdisciplinary manner. The artificial barriers are down and all skills relevant to a single project are grouped comfortably together. Follow Sheila's log a little further along to see this point about the basic skills:

> Rusty is 7½ inches long and weighs 8 ounces. We put her in a maze and it took her 3 minutes to find the food we put in one part of the maze. Then we put an alligator and 5 turtles in there with her. The turtle got along with her but the alligator didn't. He tried to bite her.
>
> Rusty's pulse is 116 because she's smaller and her blood circulates faster. Our pulse is 80 because it takes longer for our blood to circulate.

This written record represents one hour of activity. How could we classify this activity in classroom terms? Is it science, since it deals with blood circulation? Or is it mathematics, since there are elements of weighing and measuring? I detect a hint of animal psychology, human relations, spelling, and dictionary and research skills. The study undertaken by this sixth-grade youngster amply illustrates our belief that learning should be interdisciplinary, since life constantly presents problems that require an interdisciplinary approach to solve. Projects branch out to embrace whatever comes naturally. Interest in Rusty, the guinea pig in the classroom, led to

(a) problems in mathematics on how to weigh, measure, and chart growth
(b) reading to get more information
(c) art, in drawing or painting or scripting a reaction
(d) writing, to express results of research or to express a feeling
(e) moviemaking to make the story complete.

In a second-grade class, a project began by collecting interesting rocks. The rocks were classified in many ways: by color, texture, size, indestructibility, and attractiveness. Some of the rocks were weighed, measured, painted, made into decorative objects, and priced for sale. A group of children built a counter and painted a sign Rocks for Sale. Other children advertised the sale to their friends. The children acting as storekeepers found it necessary to set up a credit system since their classmates rarely carried money. The proceeds of the sale, after a hot debate, went toward a party. Several children wrote about the rock sale for the class newspaper. Many skills were learned in an interdisciplinary way as a direct result of the project. More important, each child learned that he has to call upon a combination of many skills to handle the problems of daily living.

For too long we have regarded education as preparation for living. Education for the child should be living, day by day, on his own level. We fragment and departmentalize the child's learning experience and expect him, by some miracle, to pull it all together and be able to use it in real life. This has not been successful because life is not a series of isolated disciplines. A prime example is the absence of a comprehensive body of knowledge on ecology. The physicist sees the physics of the environment, the biologist sees the biology of it, and the chemist sees the chemistry of the problem. If someone doesn't pull it all together soon and attack the totality of the environmental problem, we may not be around to worry about it.

"But how will I ever find the time to cover the curriculum?" is a question asked by many teachers in the workshops that we conduct. This is a valid question, because much valuable time and intelligent effort has been put into devising a curriculum for each subject area at every grade level. First, let us examine the reasons for writing a curriculum. A selected group of educators decides at a given time that a particular body of content is the best means by which certain skills, concepts, habits, and attitudes can be conveyed to children of a certain age. They also decide that this same body of content is a wise cultural choice for the same group of children.

What are other possibilities? Is it not possible that the same children might develop the same skills, concepts, habits, and attitudes from another body of content? Might not this other body of content be as culturally appropriate and even more relevant to the child's immediate world? Furthermore, might not an exploration and understanding of his immediate world lead the child to explore the content embracing the larger world?

A fourth-grade class in social studies studies the explorers, their countries of origin, dates of exploration, routes, and discoveries. Why? Is it because every child should know about the explorers? What does De Soto mean to him? Does he study explorers to learn what makes a person leave the security of the known to explore the challenge of the unknown? To learn what happens when an alien culture conquers an existing culture? To see how men learn to live together? To get a further appreciation of his heritage? The child can explore these questions through an in-depth study of his own changing neighborhood. When he is sufficiently interested, he could then move on to a study of De Soto. At any rate, would he grow up deprived if he never learned about De Soto?

The instructional environment of the classroom should present the child with a variety of experiences that call upon many combinations of the basic skills.

SELECTED READINGS

Books

ALMY, MILLIE, *Young Children's Thinking: Some Aspects of Piaget's Theory.* New York: Teachers College Press, Columbia University, 1966.

ARNSTEIN, FLORA J. *Poetry In The Elementary Classroom.* New York: Appleton-Century-Crofts, 1962.

Board of Education. *Teaching Literature to the Gifted.* New York: Office of Elementary Schools, 1970.

BROWN, MARY, and PRECIOUS, NORMAN. *The Integrated Day in the Primary School.* London: Ward Lock Education, 1968.

BRUNER, JEROME S. *Toward A Theory Of Instruction.* New York: Norton, 1966.

CLARIZIO, H.; CRAIG, R.; and MEHRENS, W. *Contemporary Issues in Educational Psychology.* Boston: Allyn & Bacon, 1970.

CLEGG, A. B., ed. *The Excitement of Writing.* London: Chatto & Windus (Educational) Ltd. (42 William IV Street), 1966.

DEWEY, JOHN. *Experience And Education.* New York: Collier Books (AS515), 1963.

ELKIND, DAVID. *Children And Adolescents: Interpretive Essays on Jean Piaget.* New York: Oxford University Press, 1970.

HOPKINS, LEE B. *Let Them Be Themselves.* New York: Scholastic Book Services, 1969.

LARRICK, NANCY. *A Teacher's Guide To Children's Books.* Columbus, Ohio: Charles E. Merrill, 1960.

MANN, BEATRICE F. *Learning Through Creative Work: The Under 8's in School.* Rev. ed. London: National Froebel Foundation (2 Manchester Square), 1966.

MONTESSORI, MARIA. *Dr. Montessori's Own Handbook.* New York: Schocken, 1965.

National Council of Teachers of English, *Adventuring with Books: A Reading List for the Elementary Grades.* Champaign, Ill., 1960.

PIAGET, JEAN. *The Child's Conception Of Numbers.* New York: Norton, 1965.

SACK, MARY, A., and WINTERS, S., eds. *Understanding And Teaching The Slower Student.* New York: MSS Educational, 1969.

SIGEL, I., and HOOPER, F., eds. *Logical Thinking In Children.* New York: Holt, Rinehart & Winston, 1968.

Articles

BARTH, ROLAND S. "Science: Learning Through Failure." *Elementary School Journal,* 66, no. 4 (January 1966).

BOWEN, F. H.; PAINTER, F.; and LYN, V. "Use of Recorded Music to Introduce Literature to Children." *Elementary English Review* (May 1942): 178–80.

HAWKINS, DAVID. "Messing About in Science." *Science and Children* 2, no. 5 (February 1965); *ESI Quarterly Report* 3, no. 3, (Summer and Fall 1965). (Also available in single copies as *Occasional Paper 2* from Early Childhood Education Study, Newton, Mass. 02160.)

KALLET, TONY. "Away From Stages." *Mathematics Teaching,* no. 45 (Winter 1968) . (Vine Street Chambers, Nelson, Lancastershire, England.)

———. "Some Thoughts on Children and Materials." *Mathematics Teaching,* no. 40 (Autumn 1967); also *Primary School Broadsheet,* no. 7 (Spring 1968). (Available in this country as an "Occasional Paper" from Early Childhood Education Study, 55 Chapel Street, Newton, Mass. 02160.)

———. "Some Thoughts on Integrity." *Primary School Broadsheet,* no. 5. Leicester: Leicester County Council, 1967. (Available in single copies from Early Childhood Education Study, 55 Chapel Street, Newton, Mass. 02160.)

KOBLITZ, MINNIE W. "The Negro in Schoolroom Literature." *Resource Materials for the Teacher of Kindergarten through the Sixth Grade.* New York: Center for Urban Education, 1966.

ULIN, DONALD S. "What I Learned from the British Schools." *Grade Teacher* 86, no. 6 (February 1969). (Copies of entire issue available at $1.00 each from 23 Leroy Avenue, Darien, Conn. 06820.)

Books and materials for Cuisenaire mathematics

The following books, as well as materials (i.e., classroom kit, containing rods and other materials; cubes, squares, and rods; geoboard) may be obtained from Cuisenaire Company of America, Inc., 12 Church Street, New Rochelle, New York 10805:

ANTHONY, SISTER MARIE, and JUDITH, SISTER MARY. *Discovering Truth in Numbers.* Rev. ed 1965.

DAVIDSON, JESSICA. *Using the Cuisenaire Rods.* A photo-text guide for teachers. 1970.

GALTON, G.; FAIR, A.; and DAVIDSON, P. *Student Activity Cards for Cuisenaire Rods.* 1970.

GOUTARD, MADELEINE. *Experiences with Numbers in Color in the Primary School.* Forthcoming.

KUNZ, JOHN. *Modern Mathematics Made Meaningful.* 1968.

TRIVETT, JOHN. *Mathematical Awareness.* 1962.

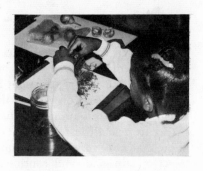

8 How Do You Grade a Total Package?

RECORD-KEEPING AND EVALUATION

Remember Henry (chapter 3), the "package deal" who comes to us with all his physical characteristics, nicer traits, problems, fears, and insecurities? The same Henry, in the course of his school career, brings home papers, tests, and report cards with strange markings on them. These markings take various forms. They may be A, A−, B+, B−, C+, C−; or 85, 80, 75, 70, 65; or √+, √++ √−. The markings are not hieroglyphics but an intricate code for grading correct answers or a final product. Do these markings give us any clue to the total package who is Henry? Do they tell us how he operates? Is he using all his capabilities? Is he happy in what he is doing? A grade of 75 may be the ultimate success for one student and total failure for another. If we believe that each child is a unique individual, then we should not use a preconceived code for rating that unique individual.

If we are truly considering using a different method of education in the classroom for part of the day or for the entire day, it is also important to consider different kinds of recordkeeping, evaluation, and reporting to parents. Since evaluation naturally flows from recordkeeping, let us first explore the various ways of keeping records. How can the teacher possibly keep track of what thirty-three children are doing if all the children are working on projects and moving freely from one activity to another? is the central question. First, let us agree that it is a physical impossibility to record everything that each child does every day. We do not attempt to do this in any method of teaching. Even if the children are sitting in neat little rows and everyone is supposedly adding 2 + 3, we know that not everyone is learning 2 + 3. To operate efficiently we have to set certain goals and routines to keep records on what we are doing as well as what the children are doing.

As soon as the children have been trained to work efficiently in the interest areas, they are asked to keep some kind of record of their daily activities. In one sixth-grade classroom, the children keep logs that include writings, graphs, charts, and pictures. A page for Sam's log looks like this:

SAM CROCODILE

11/13/69

His feelings for Rusty isn't so good and when they met face to face his mouth was open for attack. Turtles are his cousin. They're both in the reptile family. Later, in working, I hope to find out many things.

    Weight — 12 ounces
    Height — 2 inches
    Eyesight — Fair
    Skin — Soft
    Behavior to other reptiles — Fair
    Born — Unknown
    Died — Nov. 17, 1969
    Cause: Too Cold

Children's recordings of their activities take many forms. Children may tape-record their activities, note their progress on a graph or a chart, write a play or a poem, role-play, dramatize, or construct a diorama showing what they have learned. A fifth-grade nonreader who became interested in birds sculptured a perfect model of a bird to scale and was able to talk at length about the functions of the different parts of the bird's body. His talk was written down by his classmates and later incorporated into an illustrated book on birds made for the class library. He learned to read the book, and he expanded his sight vocabulary.

In the lower grades, where the laborious process of writing each day might get in the way of the learning process, the teacher may keep a class log in the form of an experience chart. This can be done easily during a sharing period.

CLASS LOG

Class 2–202   Dec. 2, 1970

José made a design on the geoboard. He counted 16 triangles. Carla put the people pieces in sets. There were 9 thin people. James worked with the balance. He found that $2 + 2 = 4$ and $2 + 3 = 5$ and $2 + 4 = 6$. Kevin, Tyrone, and Milton made a city street with blocks. Tomorrow they will put the people and cars in. Who would like to help them make people?

The class log is read and talked about. José has several important words in his story. *Design, geoboard,* and *triangles* become his words, and as he copies his story into his notebook, he underlines these important words. They are meaningful to him because he actually initiated the experience. They will become meaningful to others who are motivated by José's experience and will try the activity on another day. The next day, other children will become part of the class log, which in turn becomes a progressive record of what has been accomplished in environmental studies.

A group of second- and third-grade girls loved to dress up in the cast-off clothing kept in a carton in a corner of the classroom. The clothing was collected to aid the children in dramatization and in studying plays. These girls decided to have a fashion show. They put together their costumes very carefully and then cooperatively wrote the narration. They wanted it to be very authentic, so they brought in newspapers for the names of stores, prices, and clothing descriptions. They had to learn a whole new vocabulary, but finally they were ready. The fashion show was a great success and the narration became a permanent record of their research and results.

Making a film, which varies in difficulty from a shoebox picture film to an 8mm sound production, is an excellent way to record activities. One group of fifth-graders recorded their discoveries about birds on acetate transparencies and used the overhead projector to share them with the class. This visual record included pictures and captions. The acetate allowed some of the more difficult pictures to be traced. A first-grader made a shoebox film showing the progress his bean plant had made over a period of two weeks.

Many children can readily record their discoveries through use of the art medium, a picture story, a picture book, a bulletin-board display, or a clay model. A fourth-grade class presented a scale model of a proposed playground for the schoolyard to the principal. This model incorporated construction, painting, art decoration, and sculpting, and it was a culmination of weeks of measuring and creating play areas, analyzing existing playground construction, and interviewing children for their ideas about an ideal playground. Then the scale had to be determined;

next, materials were accumulated: toothpicks for the fence, a papertowel holder for the rocket slide, and wooden spools for the obstacle course. The model itself served as a record of the children's skills and progress.

The teacher is able to gain a great deal of insight from the children's records. First and foremost, they are a good indication of the child's true level of operation. Writing skills that must be taught are obvious; concepts that are misunderstood become evident. In this way, too, the teacher is kept aware of the children's project goals. Without imposing his own limitations upon the children's goals, he is still able to help them set realistic and attainable goals. If a child is working in only one area, it soon shows up in his recording. But can a teacher depend solely upon the children's recording to direct the learning experience? I think we would abdicate our responsibility if we did this. It is necessary for the teacher to keep records also. Some teachers set themselves the goal of writing up five children each day. As they go from group to group, they make notes on the progress of these particular children. They make sure these children participate in the sharing process for that day, so they gain further insight into their strengths and weaknesses. Most of our teachers use a form for recording, and we have as many varieties of forms as we have teachers. A typical example would be:

Date _____   Child's name _____

1. How many activities did this child engage in today?
2. What projects did (he) (she) complete?
3. What discoveries did the child make?
4. Did the child work in a group or alone?
5. Did the child require much, little, or no help?
6. Was he (she) a leader or a follower in the group?
7. Rate the child (1, 2, 3, or 4 with 1 the highest) for the following:
   Inventiveness ———
   Respect for materials ———
   Respect for opinion of others ———
   Cleanup ———
   Perseverance ———
   Ability to work in a group ———
   Accomplishments unique to this child ———
8. Comments (weaknesses, strengths, and so on): ———

Over a period of a month, each child is formally rated at least three times, and it can easily be seen if growth is taking place.

Most of our teachers keep weekly logs of the overall progress of the classroom activities. These logs have proved to be most valuable to the teachers, who record both the successes and the failures. Here are some excerpts from logs of teachers in the workshop. Some of the teachers were just getting started, while others were much further along in the program.

EXAMPLE 1: ELAINE McCANN, Grade 2 Teacher

Maryann became interested in the pan balance. She very diligently balanced marbles, checkers, beads, Styrofoam, and beans against each other. She persevered for a long time. This is another area that requires play before settling down to weighing things. The idea of balance that comes so naturally to us is a new concept for young children. I think larger weights and moderately controlled situations would be better in the beginning. Then Maryann became interested in weighing her things on a spring scale She was in no way interested in recording her findings but was willing to let me do it for her. This would be a very informative experience in number and density, the concept that two things that balance each other also weigh the same, and the necessity of keeping some sort of accurate records, and possibly setting up a table of equivalents for further use.

EXAMPLE 2: BARBARA GLICKENSTEIN, Grade 6 Teacher

We talked about our procedures for working in groups. Children were very excited about working with pets and volunteered more.

We now have a guinea pig, 5 turtles, an alligator, 2 salamanders, and 2 fish. I have collected many books, including several copies of the Zim books for identification purposes. We have scales, rulers, stopwatches, and a beautiful maze that Kenny made all by himself. Each afternoon one group would be allowed to work at the back to see how much they could find out. Each area has suggested cards that the children may or may not use.

SUGGESTION CARDS

I   *Rusty*   Born Sept. 14, 1969

   1. How old is the guinea pig?
   2. What does she weigh?
   3. How long is she?
   4. Can you describe her in words?
   5. What kind of guinea pig is she?
   6. What care is necessary to keep her healthy?
   7. What does she like to eat? How much?
   8. What sounds does she make? Why?
      Do human beings make similar sounds?
      Compare them. Use the tape recorder if you wish.
   9. How sensitive are her senses?
   10. What else can you find out?

II   *Map Area*
   1. Why do we need maps?
   2. Who makes maps?
   3. What is needed before a map can be drawn?
   4. What kind of maps are there?
   5. Can you draw a map of the classroom to scale?
   6. What kind of maps do astronauts use?

7. How far is it from Chicago to New York City?
8. Measure other distances.
9. What do the different colors on your map stand for?
10. What else can you find out?

III *Cars* (Matchbox)
1. How far does each one go?
2. Which goes further? Why?
3. What happens when they hit a barrier?
   Can you invent some safety devices to keep your car from being damaged?
4. How is your car constructed? Why?
   What is the purpose of each part?
5. How do cars and trucks pollute our air?
   What can you do about it?
6. What is the government doing about it?
7. What must you know before you can get a driver's license?
8. What else can you find out about cars?

EXAMPLE 3: BRIGITTE ROTER, Grade 3 Teacher

My first step was to arrange a table with magnets and a book explaining how they are used. I placed various types of objects on the table, some of which were attracted to magnets; others were not. My first impulse was to tell the children about this table and how it was to be used. However, before I had a chance to do so, I noticed several children wandering over to the table. I allowed them the freedom of working at the table without my direction. When I did ask them to clean up, they excitedly told me that they had worked with magnets "back there." At this time, I explained that there would be several tables set up in the back, and at given times, certain children would work at them. I also explained that all the children would get a chance to work at the tables. Therefore, they are always aware of the availability of the tables and await their turn anxiously.

My second table was composed of rocks assembled by the children after a field trip. They were very curious about the rocks and their properties. This prompted one girl to bring her rock collection to school. After discussing her rocks in terms of their shapes and colors, I presented them with a scale, magnifying glass, and a pail of water. They were on their own to discover whatever they could about their own rocks. First they weighed them, then placed them into water, weighing them again. Two girls decided to keep a record of how much each rock weighed. In order to differentiate the rocks, they labeled them according to color. Another boy rubbed the rocks together to get smaller grains and smashed them to make them even finer. In the future, I plan to make available sand and glue. My hope is that someone thinks of making sandpaper.

My third area of discovery consists of unrelated materials. I have collected objects including cardboard, beads, boxes, string, paper, buttons, paste, glue, cans, scissors. This area proved to be very fascinating. When I first put it in action, I choose two children to work at it. I left them at the table with no direction. The next five minutes overwhelmed them as they stood staring and wondering what to do with their new-found freedom. As I wondered about approaching them, I noticed that they began choosing certain objects to work with. The end result was a tin can decorated with wrapping paper fastened by paper clips and a straw placed inside, and a basket with a cardboard handle. The following two that used this area immediately began to handle the objects. One child manipulated a series of objects into different shapes and forms. At one point two rulers and a cardboard roller were held together to form a model airplane.

My plans for the future entail expanding facilities for experimentation and discovery to involve all the children at the same time. Thus far, only two or three children at a time have worked at the tables. The rest of the class was engaged in different activities. With a class of 32, I chose this gradual approach to establish the proper motivational atmosphere. Whereas, up to now, I have defined the nature and scope of the materials to be found at the discovery areas, I think that in the future these discovery areas should reflect more fully the children's interests. This can be achieved through brainstorming sessions with the class.

As teachers initiated the program in their classrooms, they wrote copious logs. The experience was so new and stimulating and the children's response so exciting that it seemed important to record every response in detail. As they became more involved with the method and used it for longer periods each week, they devised more economical ways of recording. Example 3 could have been done in this matter—

Interest Area 3   Junk Table
1. Materials provided ————; books provided ————
2. Number of children ————
3. Projects that evolved ———— complete —— incomplete ——
4. Results of sharing:
    new areas for research ————
    new vocabulary ————

It is most useful for the teacher to develop a log or file of interest areas that she can refer back to when she has a new class. This log may be as brief or as detailed as the individual teacher wishes to make it.

Thus far we have discussed the children's logs of their own interests and activities and the teacher's overall record of what has been going on in the classroom. How does the teacher evaluate the child who is learning by this method? Is it necessary for the teacher to keep some kind of record of each individual child's progress? The answer is a very definite yes. In the traditional way of teaching we keep this record in a marking book with grades, checks, crosses, and letters. In environmental education, the pupil's record is much more like the records kept in the individualized reading program. A large index card for each child filed alphabetically in an index file is one way of keeping a record. This card may be large enough for two weeks' or a month's notations, depending upon how the teacher chooses to keep his records. It should record the areas in which the child worked, the projects he completed, his weaknesses and strengths, the books he had read, new vocabulary, his self-reliance, and his ability to get along with others. It may also indicate his ability to complete home-work assignments and to learn the specific skills he needs. This very spe-cific ongoing record may be a little more work during the course of the term, but it certainly makes report-card time easier. A typical index card might look like this:

Doe, John   April 1–30

   Week of April 1: worked on puppet show. Made puppet of a clown—measured—constructed the scenery. Read 2 short plays and then children decided to write own play—helped paint the scenery.
   Observations: reads fluently—needs more practice using inches and feet—shows leadership qualities but is poor follower—new vocabulary and spelling words: *performance, circus, elephant, makeup.* Make sure he spends time in science area next week.
   Week of April 8: assigned John task card on air pressure—provided him with balloons, medicine dropper, etc., also book *Simple Science Experiments.* Worked for one hour and then we discussed results and did some reading together. He is setting up a series of experiments for that area. . . . ——

   At this point a teacher may ask, "When will I have the time to write up all these records?" Except for the weekly overall picture of the pro-gram's progress, the recordkeeping is done as the teacher moves from group to group and from child to child. If the children are motivated to work on their own at interesting projects, the teacher has time during the course of the day to write observations about individual children, obser-vations that will help her to assist that particular child to progress.
   Will the old, established report-card type of evaluations be meaning-ful in light of this new method? Can we mark a child A, B, C, or D, or 95, 85, or 65 on a project that involves a multiplicity of skills and experiences? The obvious answer is no. How then are we going to deal with reporting to parents? Two ways come immediately to mind. One would be to analyze elementary-school learning and list all the desired outcomes.

Knows how to find information	Works well with others
Attacks a problem	Works neatly
Tests his results	Is dependable
Completes a project	Shows leadership qualities

The next step would be to list the skills:

Judgments and measures	Word attack
Fractions	Comprehension
Mathematical operations	Getting the main idea
Decimals	Writing a topic sentence

The third category would be to list content areas.

This rather large, comprehensive listing would be a checklist for the entire school for the entire elementary period. The teacher could then draw upon the relevant items for her group and rate each child in every area.

Another method of reporting, used rather widely in the past few years, is the anecdotal method. The following anecdotes to parents are the result of a four-week period in which the children worked in environmental education. They all concern first-, second-, or third-grade children.

EXAMPLE 1

It took Sherri about a week to feel comfortable enough to work on projects with other children. She is very observant and loves to write. She writes well, and patiently looks up the spelling of difficult words.
Here are some of the projects she worked on:
1) She used the materials collected out-of-doors, such as seeds, pine cones, and leaves, for collage and art work. She learned the names of all the materials.
2) She made a puppet and wrote dialogue for her puppet as part of a play.
3) She painted and worked with clay.
4) She made a booklet classifying animals in various ways.

Sherri reacts very quietly to most experiences. But when she begins to write, it is evident that she has absorbed a great deal. During the next four weeks, her concentrated area will be mathematics.

EXAMPLE 2

At the beginning of this period, Christopher was uncooperative and would not accept the need for basic rules. He would go off by himself and valuable time was spent looking for him. By the middle of the second week, improvement was seen and he improved steadily from then on. By the end of the period, he accepted criticism more readily. Here are some of the projects he worked on:
1) He made a mailbox for the class post office from a flat board. He showed great patience in measuring, planning, sawing, hammering, and painting.
2) He made a puppet for the play.
3) He painted.
4) He collected fossils and made a chart identifying the fossils.
5) He showed great interest in outdoor nature study.

Christopher shows great ability to think things out for himself and to verbalize his conclusions. He progressed from total involvement with horseplay to more academic interests. His next area of concentration will be language.

EXAMPLE 3

Thomas is a quiet and kind child who shows a great deal of perseverance when working on a project that really interests him. He is willing to pursue an area of interest through to some resolution. The project that seemed to interest him the most was work with the dinosaurs. His play with the toy creatures led him to look up information in a book, draw pictures, and write captions for his pictures. Other projects included:

1) Working with geometric puzzles
2) Playing with live animals and learning about their habits, care, and feeding
3) Arts and crafts
4) Nature study

Thomas did seem rather dependent on one of the other boys in the program and should have more experience in working with groups of children. His next area of concentration will be maps and globes.

The success of the program is largely dependent upon communication with the parent. We recognize that the home is the most important environmental influence in the child's development. In selecting experiences, we should use the home and the parents as resources. Through an early meeting with the parents, we can learn a great deal about the child and can also alert the parents to special interests expressed by the child in class. The parent should know what we are going to do in the classroom and what we hope to accomplish. Our evaluation must be consistent with the goals of the program, but it must also be meaningful to the parent. Using the anecdotal method of reporting, it is also possible to tailor the evaluation to meet the specific requirements of the individual parent. For example, if a parent is particularly concerned about the child's reading, the teacher may spell out clearly the kinds of reading done, the skills mastered, the skills needed, and the help the parent can give.

In the New York City system, we have conditioned the parents to expect numerical or letter grades. Gradually we are modifying the report card to include subjective evaluations of traits to which a numerical grade cannot possibly be assigned. In many suburban areas the shift to subjective teacher evaluation is almost complete, and parents there readily accept a meaningful anecdotal evaluation in all subject areas. Parents who are kept aware of the goals of education are most willing to accept changes.

"But what about the objective performance tests?" worried teachers may ask. "The children have to score well on the Metropolitan Reading Test, on the Iowa Skills and the District Math Test, to compete with the others for entrance into the top classes in the top schools."

We fully recognize the implications of the objective performance tests in today's urban schools. We further maintain that trained teachers can use the environmental method and, at the same time, keep one eye on the tests. Materials and activities may be geared to specific vocabulary and skill development. Time may be profitably spent drilling in areas that do not arise normally in the course of open classroom exploration.

The wise teacher thoroughly familiarizes herself with her grade requirements and manages to introduce the material in a manner that is both interesting and relevant to the child. If the teacher knows that the basic reader vocabulary for the second grade includes the names of farm animals and words associated with farm living, she might use plastic models of farm animals as a turn-on agent. The children could then set up a farm situation with homes and food for the various animals. The children might record the sounds they make and put together a simple farm picture book.

We believe that the environmental approach has built-in, ongoing teacher evaluative techniques. Detailed records of children's work activities and needs should be kept by both teacher and child. When children are involved in the recordkeeping process, they have a tangible involvement in their own progress. The teacher's awareness of the children's goals and progress leads her to a continuous reevaluation of materials and activities to check their immediate relevance to the children's needs. The teacher's recordkeeping also alerts her to skills that must be taught to individuals, to small groups, and to the entire class. Teacher evaluation should exist side by side with peer evaluation, and children should be encouraged to share their activities with other groups of children. The ultimate goal for the child is honest and realistic self-evaluation.

While one teacher may keep daily records of children's accomplishments on a wall chart, another may keep an anecdotal log. Another teacher prefers a weekly summary of directions, accomplishments, and problems, leading to a periodic overall evaluation. There is a variety of methods for the individual teacher to choose from.

PART II

Educational Roles

9 A Child Is a Child, and That Is Nice!

THE ROLE OF THE CHILD

Roles are very much discussed these days. People often speak of the professional role one fulfills. If a person is a lawyer, he is expected to handle legal matters, not to diagnose physical illnesses, which is a doctor's role. If he is a medical doctor and a lawyer, then he can be expected to diagnose patients, but he has to make it clear that he is acting in his medical, not his legal, role. Therefore, most firms have "job descriptions" to define the role or roles one fills in a particular company.

Psychotherapists usually speak of roles in a nonprofessional sense. The mother who tries to be only a "pal" to her daugher is said to have a confused role. Since she is the mother, she ought to be kind, understanding, and open, and she must also fill the roles urged upon her by the natural condition of motherhood, such as her authoritative role. Confused roles bring confusion both to the person not filling the role and to the person subjected to the false role-playing. So it seems worthwhile to specify in detail the roles of the principal agents in the environmental method we are advocating.

But before we do—do you recall Willie Sutton? He became rather well-known during the 1960s. A notorious bank robber who had gone unapprehended for many years, Willie Sutton was finally captured by the police. However, he was not caught in the act of robbing another bank. The police simply came up beside Willie quietly while he was strolling down a neighborhood street in New York's lower Manhattan apparently with no thought of safecracking.

After Willie was booked, officials decided that he should have a psychiatric examination prior to his trial. From the newspaper accounts, there was no reason to doubt Sutton's sanity, unless one believes a priori that anyone who robbed as many banks as Willie did must at least be *suspected* of being psychologically ill. That all of these robberies had been successfully accomplished with physical injury to no one evidently did not speak in favor of Willie Sutton's sanity. Anyone who continuously robs banks may be a compulsive psychotic—this seems to have been the thinking.

As reported, the doctor began the examination with the usual preliminary questions: name, age, and so on. Eventually the doctor inquired why Willie had robbed so many banks. Why had he, so to speak, made bank-robbing the major objective of his life? In a reply that is classically brief, simple, and clear-minded, Willie answered, "Because that's where they keep the money, and I wanted money."

If you want money, go where the money is kept. Needless to say, Willie Sutton's sanity was established and so was his guilt. He was convicted and sent to prison. To finish the story, serious illness aggravated by the complications of old age brought about Willie's release long before he served his full term.

All of us should be as single-minded about education as Willie Sutton was about bank-robbing. For whose benefit does an elementary education exist? The child's benefit, of course; we want to educate the *children*. In the educational process, they ought to be the main focus of our attention. Why don't we, with single-minded purpose, steadfastly keep our minds and efforts focused on helping children to learn? It should be as simple as that, but what happens in practice? All too frequently many other demands cry out for attention. Educators are distracted from the real business at hand, and they confuse issues and falsify roles. The tragicomic side of this, moreover, is that almost all of the overwhelming, distracting demands are made in the name of better education for the children. But the actual result is that all too frequently the most effective methods for teaching the child are bypassed, buried, rejected, or emasculated for reasons that are not concerned, when honestly analyzed, with what is best for the child, but with extraneous and sometimes irrelevant factors. What these factors are—sometimes political, sometimes personal, and sometimes economic—we shall not consider here. Simply realize that this paradox would not occur if all of us involved in educating children remained single-minded in our intentions to give the children the most effective opportunities for learning successfully, and if each district superintendent, principal, teacher, and parent, fulfilled this role properly.

If you agree with what we have said so far in this book, then you should also agree that elementary education ought to be child-centered; that the concentrated and coordinated efforts of all the other agents involved—parents and politicians, educational administrators and the community, teachers and teachers' unions—ought to see to it that the children are provided with what is best for their education. Everyone must fill the roles that work toward this goal. If roles are falsified, confused, or neglected, the child suffers.

There are people of all kinds—teachers, parents, educational administrators, and philosophers of education—who bristle at the expression "child-centered education." To them, "child-centered" means that the educator indulges the child. They envision overpermissive teachers allowing children to behave self-indulgently, and teachers having only one concern, namely, not to place any demands whatsoever on the children. As you have already gathered in this book, this is not our meaning of "child-centered." On the contrary, the child has a definite role to play in our method. The child is the *principal agent in the learning process,* as was explained in the chapters on the psychological and social environment. But to say that the child is the *principal agent* in the learning process does not mean that he must be self-indulged, nor does it minimize the important role of the teacher or downgrade the role of the educational administrators, parents, and the community. The child performs his role as the principal agent in the learning process best when the others perform their roles most effectively. They are needed, and their help is invaluable, but ultimately, learning *takes place in the child.* He is the learner. We can teach him, but we can't "learn" him. He has to want, at least to some extent, to learn. He has to do the thinking, and this is what we must focus on.

The child's fundamental role is to learn and to learn how to learn; these, of course, are two sides of one coin. There are many things the child should learn, but the most necessary and most useful thing for him to learn is the effective *way* to learn. Neither the teacher nor the child can determine a priori how the child learns arithmetic, spelling, writing, geography, art, or whatever, in the best way. The child needs the freedom to explore different ways of learning. The purpose of the exploration is not "to allow the child to do whatever he feels like." The purpose of the exploration is for the child to discover through trial and error his latent or developing personal traits, talents, and learning style, with the *sustaining and directing help of the teacher.*

Therefore, incorrect answers, failures, and mistakes must not be experienced by the child as indications of stupidity. The role of the child is to see why his answer in arithmetic is incorrect, or why he made a mistake in spelling, or why his experiment in trying to make a bell ring by wiring it to a battery, failed. What did he do wrong? What did he do incorrectly? How can he learn it correctly? What method helps him best to learn it correctly? If one method fails, he must try another. His role is to be active, because he is the principal agent in the learning process. Adelaide, Bernard, Carmen, David, or any other pupil will not play the role of learner, however, unless they are interested and motivated.

Though interest and motivation can be elicited by another person, they ultimately happen within the child. They cannot be turned on automatically the way an electric lightbulb in a lamp is turned on by the switch. A teacher can try to interest or motivate the child, but, as teachers know very well, they do not always succeed in their attempts to win the children's attention. It is, at best, a tricky and unpredictable enterprise. Even when teachers discover what interests a child most of the time, they cannot be sure it will continue to interest that child. To compound the problem, what interests one child now may turn off most of the other children at the same time.

However, interest is a problem that we cannot ignore. It is there as clearly as the physical presence of the children in the classroom. Unless you win the children's attention and interest, you are wasting your time trying to teach them. Their young minds may be elsewhere. The children may be sitting up in their seats, heads forward, innocent eyes gazing dreamily at you, all as quiet as dolls in a toy store, and paying just as much attention. A person passing by such a classroom and peeking in to see what is going on might think that the teacher is presenting an excellent, clear, and well-thought-out lesson, and that all the heads are absorbing it like little round sponges. Actually, their minds may be in fantasyland.

Of course, sometimes the lack of interest is painfully obvious. Mary is whispering to Nancy; Oliver has begun to punch Paul who sits next to him; Quentin has begun to wander about the room with that vacant look on his face. Will shouting get their attention? An experienced teacher knows that in the long run, shouting is the least effective way of getting attention. Shall I be soft-spoken but firm, and bring each of the inattentive pupils, whether quiet or disruptive, to attention? But even if I succeed now, how long will I have their attention?

Superior teachers, no matter what method they use, are superior by their talent—inventive, if not always strictly creative—to win the interest and motivation of their students. They break the bonds of the very formal and highly structured formats of the boring classroom routines. In so doing, they innovate in their own way, and for this they deserve only the highest praise. In suggesting that the method we propose allows for greater opportunities to stimulate the child's interest and motivation, we do not wish to denigrate the superb results superior teachers achieve within the more traditional framework. Quite the contrary—the fact that these teachers have succeeded shows that they have discovered the master key to the children's minds: interest and motivation. They have recognized the central fact that the child is the learner, and that they must first stimulate his interest and motivation.

We are suggesting that since the child is the principal agent of the learning process the most important question is, What actually turns this child on? What captures his interest here and now and motivates him to learn? A teacher cannot take the reverse attitude, confusing the role of the teacher with the role of the pupil. If I am to succeed with this child, it is foolish to think that this child, this group of children, or this class *ought* to be interested and motivated in a certain thing, that a reasonable child *should* respond properly to a worthy interest.

The question is not what we adults, with our own value systems, backgrounds, likes, and dislikes, think ought to and should interest and motivate the child. The proper question is not what motivated us when we were children, either. Furthermore, the real issue is not, as some teachers pose it, that the children were not brought up properly and trained to pay attention, that they should have learned respect for their teacher.

The only real question with which we can deal in a practical and constructive manner if we wish to help the children is what interests and motivates this particular child? We must start with the factual situation. The child's role is to become interested, but apart from coercion, which never succeeds, I am left with only one alternative: I must discover the child's genuine interest. I can then capitalize on the child's interest to channel him into a learning experience—no matter how simple—where he can succeed. The success, in turn, motivates the child to continue and to pursue a new interest, which leads to another learning experience. Here is where the perception, maturity, and expertise of the teacher helps guide the child to profitable learning experiences.

An example may help at this point: A woman who was attending our workshops, was a tradition-oriented teacher. Accustomed at one time to pupils who came from families of high achievers and were high achievers themselves, she had found little difficulty in motivating them. Times changed, the neighborhood changed, and the makeup of the school population changed. Now this teacher is faced with more than a few disinterested, disruptive, low-achieving pupils. When this change had started, she thought that strong and swift discipline would win the battle.

At the workshop-seminars, she argued eloquently against what we have proposed in this book. But things became so difficult in her classroom that she decided one day to try what we proposed. One of her pupils, James, had been bringing a matchbox car to class every day. He played with it constantly. He ran it across the top of the desk and created distracting sounds that caught the attention of the other children. Holding it in his hands sometimes, he spun the wheels. In a word, James's inventiveness in playing with the matchbox car was quite extraordinary, and quite exasperating for the teacher in a number of ways.

In the past, this teacher had punished James in an equally inventive number of ways. A matchbox car still appeared with James each day. The point of utter frustration came. What to do? Try to capitalize on James's interest? After all, he must be interested in matchbox cars because he always has one with him. Instead of punishing James, she spoke to James in the front of the room this time: "James, do you like matchbox cars?"

"Yeah."

"Would you like to tell the class something about matchbox cars and why you like them?"

Hesitant at first, James began to talk. His interest bubbled out; James saw that he had the interest of his fellow pupils, and he felt flattered and elated, which encouraged him to say more. When he was finished, the teacher asked James if he would like to do a little project on matchbox cars. Maybe he would like to explain different models, or measure them, or compare a specific model to a real car, or find out the metals from which they are made and how they are made. James was delighted. Once the disruptive "loser" in the class, he became the "winner." He told his teacher he would explain different models in the next class and would do the other work, too.

By capitalizing on this interest, the teacher was able, little by little, to steer James in more profitable learning experiences. No longer was he disruptive; now he had interest and motivation. Most of all, he had experienced some success and the good will of his classmates. Here, as you can see, the role of the teacher was to prepare the environment, to set up the conditions that permitted James to focus on something that truly interested him. James moved into his role and pursued his interest. The teacher then followed up her role, and with suggestions and commendations she guided James into more and more profitable learning experiences. Had this teacher continued to reject matchbox cars as improper for a classroom environment, James would have become unmanageably explosive. Then what would be done to help James?

Some teachers have a number of objections at this point, and we have indeed heard them at many workshops. They are too well-founded in fact to be ignored. Some teachers have called notice to the brief span of attention of their pupils. Others have quoted the number of low-achievers, educational failures, and discipline problems they have in their particular classes. Others point out that many of their pupils are too thoughtless, noisy, hostile, and undisciplined to be able to pursue their individual or collective interests. "What they need most is good, strong discipline" we frequently hear. Finally, not a few teachers have told us,

"Don't you realize that most children, especially the very young, do not know what they want or what they are interested in? They flit like butterflies from one interest to another! To cater to their whims is to chase soap bubbles. You have to insist that they pay attention to what they must learn. What you talk about is beautiful and idealistic, but it would never work in my classroom."

Having visited a large number of classrooms in many different schools, and having discussed these matters with an extensive number of teachers, we have become acutely aware of the wide differences among pupils and classroom problems. We are also aware of how disruptive, destructive, and even violently dangerous, some young children can be. No method of education, we are convinced, can handle all of these problems successfully. At times, the solutions to some of these problems are not in the hands of the teachers. In such cases the teacher may be fulfilling his role perfectly, but administrators, the city fathers, the federal government, or whatever, may be failing in its role to provide the proper facilities, services, personnel or something else.

We are aware that the method we are proposing is not the solution to all classroom problems. It is not a method that will always guarantee success. In our view, its value lies in the fact that it does prove to be successful in many cases that at present are unsuccessful learning situations. That is sufficient reason, we believe, why it should be given a chance in situations where it could be helpful. Support for this position is based on solid experience: we have seen startling transformations of children's classroom behavior, including some older sixth-grade children, where this method was introduced.

Let's be honest—many times the reason why children are disruptive and destructive in school is that they are not interested in what they are supposed to learn. Not infrequently, what the teacher proposes to teach, and more importantly, the manner in which he presents it, has little or no meaning in many children's lives. Maybe it should have, ought to have, meaning for them, but what if it doesn't? Are they required to sit still and be quiet while they suppress stored-up energy, which goes nowhere? Children have a natural urge to be active, to do something. But if what the teacher is saying is as foreign to them as an occult language, they cannot put their imaginations, minds, or bodily powers to work on it. The energy is there, however, and it builds up like steam in a closed vessel. Then comes the explosive moment, and disruption or destruction takes place. If that energy had been channeled from the start into some constructive and successful activity, there would have been little or no reprehensible behavior.

One of the teachers who participated in our program had the lowest exponent of the sixth grade in an extremely disadvantaged school. He was deeply disturbed by the attitude and behavior of his pupils; he saw no solution to the problem. When we proposed to him, one day at the workshop, that he should allow these youngsters to choose projects in which they would be interested, his reply was quick and sure: "They are interested in nothing. They lack all initiative and basic skills. They are physically overactive and undisciplined. If I allowed them to work on projects, they would just fool around with the materials and would probably throw the materials at one another. Even if they started some projects, they would never continue them. They would quickly lose interest and cause trouble."

That was quite an indictment. We told him that if the situation was as desperate as he described, he must be spending all his time on discipline, not on teaching. This he readily admitted. We suggested that perhaps these children needed an outlet more than most other children, so why not give them a chance? He agreed to do so. We urged the following cautions:

1. Trust these children. Be confident that they can be interested in something.
2. Be open from the start to what interests them.
3. Accept their interests, even if at this stage their interests are not connected with the curriculum.
4. Set down a few clear directives of what will and will not be tolerated in class. Explain the reasons for these directives and discuss them with the youngsters to win their understanding and cooperation in meeting the directives. This makes their role clear in the classroom.
5. Be patient. Don't expect miracles. Build slowly on interests. Spend all the time necessary on basic skills.
6. Make sure that they have success in their initial undertakings. They have had too many experiences of failure. Their self-image is negative, and it has to be changed slowly into a positive self-image.
7. Lead the individual pupils gradually to more challenging educational experiences.
8. Don't panic about the curriculum. They were not learning the content of the curriculum with your previous method. You can work on the curriculum when they have developed adequate interest and motivation.

What were the results? Some of the boys, older than most sixth-graders, were rough and aggressive and wanted to work with such simple equipment as electric batteries, bulbs, and bells. They had never had the opportunity before "to fool around and see how they work." Here was not a lesson, but a chance to find out about things they were interested in. Other boys wanted to build a speedway for small racing cars. A few wanted to work with art materials, and so it went. The girls' interests went in other directions. Some wanted to compare different kinds of dress and clothing materials, and find out what the materials were made of. Another group wanted to make biscuits and pancakes. Individual girls pursued projects that centered on cosmetics and makeup in general, drawing, and needlework.

The whole class became interested in their projects. Slowly and patiently, the teacher led them from the initial interest to further explorations. He combined traditional teaching with project periods. The classroom was alive; students were active. The noise level rose at times, but following the directives set up by the pupils themselves, the boy in charge rang the bell, which was the signal for all to stop and lower the noise level. All the physical energy that formerly went into disruptive activity now went into planned activities. The pupils got to be friendly and cooperative. The remarkable change that came over them we witnessed at first hand. The teacher is now an ardent and practiced partisan of this approach.

It is important to add that the role of the child is not only to learn how to learn and to learn necessary skills, but also to learn helpful social behavior. This role, however, cannot be learned by the child in the classroom unless the environment there not only permits, but positively encourages the child to associate with and develop good relationships with the other children. The teacher must let the children know clearly what their "social" roles are. Simple explanations, discussions, talking things over, private corrections of individuals, all should be part of the classroom procedures. Thoughtfulness toward others, cooperative action, sharing, regard for others' privacy, respect for one another's opinions, acceptance of one another's ethnic background—these are things children have to learn. Like all learning, it has to take place in them. Experience in social relationships has the same essential dynamics as other learning experiences. Successes help one to learn the right way; failures should be used as learning experiences, too, to correct mistakes and see what went wrong.

This, indeed, is discipline. Discipline is not an end in itself. It is not aimed at keeping children quiet and still. Discipline is not intended to frighten children into learning and does not dominate by fear. It is not a discipline that covers up the neurotic insecurity of an inwardly distrusting and threatened person. Rather, discipline is a means to achieve constructive personal and social behavior. It is a way in which an adult can help a child to fulfill himself and allow others equally to fulfill themselves.

Eric Fromm and a host of other psychotherapists have pointed out the need for all humans to learn "the art of loving." We must learn how to love from our earliest years, or we grow up as emotional cripples. People knowing neither the meaning or experience of love, nor how to love, fail to give and receive love. Similarly, children must learn the art of self-discipline, of internal discipline without which healthy social behavior and the art of loving others are impossible. The role of the child is not to be socially mature; rather, the role of the child is to have the opportunity, the guidance, and the help to grow daily in becoming socially more responsible. Only by such a gradual process can the child develop into a socially mature adult. This requires trust in the child, warm acceptance of him as an individual person, clear and purposive directives, and patience with his mistakes.

In a nutshell, self-discipline requires a learning process. On the other hand, discipline that is limited to rigid, external regulations and measured only in terms of conformity and nonconformity is admittedly a conditioning process. It can at times be notably successful in obtaining external conformity. Some teachers feel safe with the conviction that they have the whole class constantly under control, but is this the object of education? If our aim is to help the child as the principal agent in the educational process, is this rigid kind of discipline really helping the child, or is it guaranteeing the teacher temporary security?

We have not become softhearted to the point of becoming soft-headed. The following items are *not* the role of the child in the classroom. No child, no matter how young or old, should be permitted to do what he pleases, as he pleases, and when he pleases, contrary to clear directions. No child should be permitted to put on temper tantrums to get his own way. A child who bullies other children or tries to bully the teacher is obviously out of order. Children must be prevented from doing physical harm to other children. The child who belittles another child's race or ethnic or religious background needs positive and helpful correction. We are all agreed that there are limits to what the child should be permitted to do.

Children must learn to behave properly, but within tolerable limits. Let us repeat that last phrase, *within tolerable limits,* because we want to refine it further. *Limits* indicates that there must be clear simple, purposive directives stating what is forbidden, but within the performance capabilities of the child or children in question. *Tolerable* calls our attention to the fact that we must, as adults, continuously keep in mind that they are children—not miniature adults, not adult midgets, not small-sized models of ourselves. As children at a particular age level, they have definite physical and psychological weaknesses in communicating, thinking, keeping still, and in dealing with their emotions. "A child is a child is a child," to misquote Gertrude Stein. We must realize that they will behave like children, and not necessarily "like good little children," but like children—with a great deal of irresponsibility, animal spirits, forgetfulness, distraction, kindness, meanness, generosity, and almost crude selfishness.

We must tolerate a great deal. We must be tolerant as we help them to grow in and through all the strengths and weaknesses that make childhood what it is. Limits we must set, but they must be in accord with the child's development and rate of growth, and they must be as few as are needed. They must be clear and purposive, not arbitrary or whimsical, and they must be held to. If they are proper limits, they are only for the child's good. To neglect proper limits is to allow the child to be hurt.

One of the authors shall never forget the best experience he has had of witnessing how children can be taught to behave properly within tolerable limits. A few years ago he had the good fortune to be asked to work on a research team to study the children of some Navaho families on a reservation in northern New Mexico. When the members of this team first got to know each of the families, he was surprised at the closeness of the children to their parents, the freedom with which they played, the tolerance that the adults showed the children, and the warmth of feeling they shared with them. The first impression was one of permissiveness on the part of the adults. Yet the children did not seem to overstep the privileges that any mature and wise adult would grant to children.

How to explain this wonderful phenomenon? It was only after some time and very close contact with these families that the members of the team discovered that there were limits set to the children's behavior. They were tolerable limits, well-defined and strictly adhered to. Unless these limits were violated, the adults accepted with warm tranquility and without interference the noisy play, the plaintive cries, the minor altercations between the children of the extended family group, the falls and minor cuts and bruises, the angry words of the boys to one another, the silly laughter of the little girls, the running into the hogan to fetch something to eat—in a word, all the behavior of the children short of what was clearly forbidden. These Navaho people, who possessed such a remarkable affinity with nature, had a very admirable awareness of growth. They knew the laws of growth; they knew that children were in the process of growth. One must be patient with growth. One waits for the tree to grow; one waits for the dawn to come in order to have light. Sundown brings darkness and the night. One learns to be patient and to allow things the time that is due them. Each season has its own span of time, and so do the seasons of human life.

What about teaching the child responsibility? Can we teach the child responsibility if we do not grant him sufficient freedom within which he can learn responsibility? I'm afraid that more than a few adults, among them an average number of teachers, think of children as too young and inexperienced to be allowed a freedom commensurate with their growth. Somehow they expect the child to develop the responsibility for freedom without having had a freedom in which to learn to exercise proper responsibility. Is responsibility something you teach a child from the outside, or is it something the child must also learn through the experience of exercising responsibility? Is responsibility a charismatic gift that suddenly comes from out of the blue and descends on the child to prepare him for freedom? The fact is that the child has to learn day by day how to use freedom and at the same time to exercise responsibility. (Remember, the child is the principal agent in the learning process.) Responsibility cannot be learned solely by explanations to the children. Explanations and discussions must be followed by actual experiences. Will there be mistakes and failures? Of course there will. Is the teacher taking a chance? Isn't it better to make sure that the child is absolutely protected at all times?

If the last refrain sounds like an overprotective mother, remember that there can be teachers who for various reasons are overprotective, too. They confuse their role, which is to help the child to learn, with the child's role. They try to take over the child's role and use their experience and knowledge to prevent the child from making any mistakes. But how does the child ever get to fulfill his role as the principal agent of his learning process?

We have heard teachers say at our workshops, "I would never let any child use a scissors in my classroom. He might cut himself or injure another child." (If with due precautions a child is never permitted to use a scissors, how does he get to learn to use one?) "No child in my class will be allowed Cuisenaire rods. They might swallow the small rods or throw the big ones at the other children and injure someone." (Does it bother that teacher that some children learn math most quickly and best with these rods?) "As long as I have the responsibility for my pupils, I will not permit any child in my class (fourth grade) to use a hammer or a saw. They could easily hurt themselves." (Some "discipline-problem" boys are amazingly turned on to mathematics and science, then to reading and social studies, by letting them build something.)

The child has to work within some small area of freedom and responsibility every day so that he can learn by his mistakes and failures as well as by his successes. The role of the child is to learn how to become a genuinely self-directing person capable of exercising freedom and social responsibility. This he has to learn in the classroom as well as in the home and in the community. But how can he, unless the environment of the classroom promotes and warmly encourages him day by day?

Remember Willie Sutton. Be single-minded and child-centered, and do not confuse roles. Know the role of the child and allow him the freedom and the responsibility to fulfill his role. Make him the principal agent of his learning process. Capitalize on his interest and motivation. Let him learn discipline, an internal discipline commensurate to his rate of growth. Let him learn to be a socially responsible person in a socially responsive environment.

SELECTED READINGS

Books

FRAIBERG, SELMA H. *The Magic Years.* New York: Scribner (SL-161), 1959.

HENTOFF, NAT. *Our Children are Dying.* New York: Viking (Compass Book C-210), 1966.

OREM, R. C., ed. *Montessori and the Special Child.* New York: Putnam, 1969.

REDL, FRITZ. *When We Deal with Children.* New York: Free Press, 1966.

SEARS, P., and SHERMAN, V. *In Pursuit of Self-Esteem: Case Studies of Eight Elementary School Children.* Belmont, Calif.: Wadsworth, 1964.

STRANG, RUTH. *An Introduction to Child Study.* 4th ed. New York: Macmillan, 1959.

10 1 Teacher = 1 Knowing Mind + 1 Loving Heart + 2 Helping Hands

THE ROLE OF THE TEACHER

How does the role of the teacher in the informal classroom differ from the role of the teacher in the formally structured classroom? To answer this question, it is necessary to first examine the roles of the teacher in today's city classrooms. Many teachers find this question of role definition most difficult. Is the elementary-school teacher primarily an educator or a combination of substitute mother, doctor, nurse, tailor, janitor, judge, and jury?

Think of a typical, formal third-grade teacher's morning. She arrives at least a half hour before the children, tidies the room, checks the shades, and waters the plants. She changes the date on the calendar, puts the plan for the day on the board, and assembles the materials necessary for the day's work. The children arrive, hang up their coats, take their seats, and prepare to *receive* the day's lessons. All is in order, but Jane is crying because she fell and skinned her knee in the schoolyard, Tommy has a toothache for the third day, and Michael has his usual morning stomachache due to coming to school without breakfast. Peter cannot get his boots off—they are stuck, half-on, half-off. Carol has accused Linda of stealing her pencil, and a fight is imminent if a judgment is not made promptly. Florence has to have a note permitting her to be dismissed early to go to the doctor. A note has to be sent to Keith's mother, informing her that the school pictures must either be paid for or returned. Meanwhile Marvin spills his milk and the mess has to be cleaned up immediately.

This is a typical uneventful morning with no unusual crises. Are the teacher's roles coming through loud and clear? Her role is to set up the physical environment of the room, impart or cover the day's educational content, comfort Jane and administer first aid, contact the proper authorities to see that Tommy gets to see a dentist, provide Michael with some milk and cookies, help Peter with his boots, find Carol's pencil or provide another one, write Florence's note, and contact Keith's mother. Along the way, she also has to supervise the mopping-up of the spilled milk. No wonder so many teachers come home at the end of the day drained of energy, and so many others just let everything go to the point of chaos.

In this teacher-centered classroom, the teacher has assumed all the roles. This total assumption of the roles has resulted in an exhausted teacher who too often gets so bogged down that the true business of the classroom, helping each child to grow and advance, gets lost in the shuffle. The teacher in the teacher-centered classroom tends to overlook her greatest help and asset, the children themselves. In the example above, the teacher has had to postpone the problems of teaching for the immediate problems of living, and the uninvolved children are passively waiting for her to get around to the business of teaching.

In the child-centered classroom, learning is a part of living, and the children are actively engaged in the process of living and learning from the moment they come into the classroom. As long as the children are actively engaged in projects of their own choosing and are helping each other, the teacher is free to pursue her many roles in the classroom in a much more relaxed and less pressured manner. Of course, emergencies are handled first, and a skinned knee is treated promptly. Children help each other with their outer clothing and help themselves to milk and cookies. Pencils and materials are readily available for all the children, and routines are set up for their use and sharing.

In the informal classroom, the first role of the teacher is to set up a physical environment that promotes the optimal participation by all the children in the learning experience. An environment conducive to learning is one in which all materials are readily accessible, guidelines and limitations are clearly spelled out, and duties and responsibilities are delineated. This kind of setup takes planning, discussion, and constant evaluation *with the children*. Plan with the children to satisfy their needs, discuss with the children to determine their interests and set their goals, and evaluate with the children to foster self-evaluation and internal discipline.

Once the initial physical environment is set up, the teacher's second role is to learn how to get out of the way of learning. Too often a teacher stifles a child's natural curiosity and initiative with too many questions, too many demands, and too many judgments. A child who is hesitant about trying things on his own is stopped cold when a teacher judges his efforts as wrong or incorrect. He may have surmised that all is not quite right, and he may be about to try another way, when the teacher places the kiss of death upon his tentative efforts. Give the child time to explore on his own, and step in only when the child has exhausted his own initiative. Be patient with the child who has to try the same thing over and over. He is learning.

Teachers who have taught for many years tend to become fixed in their habits, and they impose these fixed habits upon their pupils. "Penmanship paper must be folded into three columns, and the words must be written across the page." Why must this be done? Because this is "the way it is done," or "the way we have always done it." It is important to let the child find ways of doing things himself. His way may turn out to be more relevant to his needs or more indicative of his true level of operation than a teacher's fixed, imposed method. There is always a chance too that the child may give us insights into better, more efficient ways of doing things.

Another advantage of getting out of the way of learning is that the teacher no longer has to invent contrived motivations for irrelevant lessons. The classroom is set up for a vital learning situation. The motivation is built into the materials and the situations. Children stimulate one another, report to one another, and share with one another. This moves the teacher from the center stage to the wings perhaps, and places the children all over the stage, where they rightfully belong.

We have stated in a previous chapter our conviction that the teacher is a very important and necessary person in the classroom. He is most important in his third role, a facilitator of learning, because he is the greatest single resource person in the classroom by virtue of his experience, his educational background, and his training for his profession. A teacher cannot make a child learn or give a child learning—he can only make it easier or more pleasant for the child to acquire learning. This means developing a sensitivity to Henry's needs. Is this a good time to let Henry explore by himself, or is it a time to step in with a question or a suggestion? Has Henry succeeded in choosing a balanced educational diet for this week, or is it time to steer Henry in a specific direction? What materials can I provide for Sam so that he can go ahead with his experiment. Susan gives up very easily and needs a series of successful short-term experiences to build up her confidence. What projects will provide the success she needs in order to facilitate her learning process?

The teacher must consider every child's needs. He cannot do this from center stage while busily pulling all the strings. He can do this easily from the wings, while the children are to some extent actively directing themselves and each other. If he is to assist the child in acquiring a balanced educational diet, he has to steer his classroom between the Scylla of leaving the children loose and completely undirected and the Charybdis of the teacher-dominated classroom. If he is alert, aware, sensitive, and has developed the talent of listening carefully to his children, he can structure his classroom, through periodic changes in the physical setup and changes in the materials, to meet the current needs of the children.

The fourth role of the teacher in the informal classroom is to grow and expand himself. We envision new dimensions for the classroom teacher who is involved in environmental education. No longer are teachers cast into a single mold. This method of education is most adaptable to the teacher's personality and style. The teacher is removed from center stage in the classroom, yet the program may well reflect his personal interests, strengths, or hobbies. Our program is child-centered without diminishing the role of the teacher. He has the freedom to allow his own imagination, abilities, and natural talents to operate in innovative paths. If he is a gourmet cook, the interest in cooking may be the turn-on agent for many open-ended experiences leading to measuring skills, studies of different cultures, foods, diets, geography, reading, and literature. As a result of his own interest and proficiency, he naturally communicates his enthusiasm to the children. An atmosphere of mutual interest, trust, and respect, is created when both teacher and pupils are turned on to and involved in the learning process. In this atmosphere, both are free to explore and grow.

However, the teacher's own interest and proficiencies may not suffice to stimulate the children. He must be prepared to explore unknown paths and byways with the children, to admit that he does not know the answers, and to grow with his pupils. This is difficult for many teachers who feel that they must know all the answers, but an all-knowing teacher creates a false situation in any classroom. (With the great explosion of knowledge in the last century, who could possibly know all the answers?) The teacher, however, by reason of his experience and expertise, is able to direct the children to find the answers, and this is the key to his fourth role in the classroom.

A fifth role of the teacher is to help the child become aware of the power he exerts by his own learning process—in short, to help the child become independent and self-reliant in the classroom. Here again, this is most difficult. Many teachers enjoy subjugating the children: "Fold your hands"; "Stand in a straight line"; "Don't touch the paper until I tell you how to do it." We thereby neglect the development of the child's self-reliance in the ordinary classroom, yet it is probably the single most useful power that the child can develop. "If I try several alternatives, I can probably succeed in finding out how to do it myself" is the crowning statement of a child's learning experience. This child has learned how to learn. In so doing, he has cut down a great deal of his dependence upon the teacher.

Basic to this approach is the philosophy that children are individual human beings who are capable of becoming actively involved in their own learning and are capable of employing self-initiation and self-direction. A teacher who subscribes to this philosophy soon gets to know the children well, for when a child is involved in doing something, then teacher and child have a basis for discussion. Knowledge of the child's interest and concerns enables the teacher to act as a catalytic agent, a hurdle-jumper, and a resource person. He must also be able to hold back and encourage children to help each other. He may refer a child who is having difficulty printing on fabric to one who has been successful doing it. Many teachers use this technique, realizing that it is often easier for children to communicate with one other than with an adult. As the child discovers, the teacher accepts the child's efforts and offers encouragement leading to the child's feeling of accomplishment and satisfaction. If the child needs a particular skill in order to advance to a new level of achievement in his area of interest, the teacher is alert to the need and is available to teach the skill. If the child goes off in a completely unanticipated direction, a direction in which the teacher himself feels insecure, here is an opportunity to encourage, explore, and learn together.

An important part of the teacher's role is to structure the learning process through the selection and presentation of a wealth of varied workable materials, experiences, and trips. On the one hand, we are looking to capitalize on materials and experiences from the child's own immediate environment; on the other hand, we want to provide experiences that enable the child to explore beyond his environment.

To initate the program in the classroom, the teacher may very well plan upon introducing a group of experiences based upon an interest of his own or of the children. It is necessary for the teacher to experiment with the materials and to anticipate the possible paths they might lead to. If the children are turned on by the initial presentation, then it is a valuable experience to pursue.

Not all children will be turned on by the same experience. The good teacher should be aware of the individual differences in work cycles and emotional states of the children in her class. If the turn-on agent is fabrics, and the child has expressed interest in animals, he might investigate sheep and silkworms to make his contribution. If he is tired or upset, he should feel free to pursue an activity that will satisfy his needs for that day. When interest lags, the teacher must be sensitive enough to introduce new materials.

Assuming the Socratic proposition that no teacher can teach another person anything but can only expose a pupil to certain stimuli and facilitate the learning process, let us go back and consider some of the basic questions posed by teachers attending the environmental studies workshop.

If we move toward a more child-centered classroom, with the child participating in the initiation of his own learning, are we, by so doing, diminishing the role of the teacher in the classroom? Absolutely not. We are, in truth, changing the role of the teacher, but we are in no way lessening his function. He remains the interested, compassionate, creative, resourceful adult, the single most important person in the classroom. His role extends from giver of information to guide, helper, creator, and confidant. He meets the child on many levels in terms of his individual hopes, concerns, interests, fears, goals, and aspirations. He is better able to choose the materials and learning experiences best suited to each child because he comes to know the children better. He is constantly learning along with the children as their natural curiosity leads them into ever-expanding areas.

Must a teacher abandon all his former ways of teaching to adopt this newer and different method? Again the answer is no. Teachers in our workshops have demonstrated the effectiveness of this method as a partial program over and over again. Their individual time schedules for the program vary from one afternoon a week to every afternoon, to three full days a week, to all day every day. Gradually this method of learning seems to take over even the formal lessons because once children are exposed and trained to participate in their own learning, they use this skill in every type of lesson.

Two elements disappear from the classroom: anxiety about failure and competitiveness. If a teacher teaches a formal math lesson to the entire class and then gives the class some problems to solve, the children help each other and accept help naturally because they have become accustomed to group interplay and stimulation. Children are also motivated to complete their textbook and work book exercises so that they can continue their own projects. They come to see the necessity for learning certain skills to further their abilities.

The teacher's old ways of teaching are gradually modified but not abandoned. In all cases, the children seem to move easily from free-flowing, self-initiated work in individual or group projects, to whole-class formal lessons without any difficulty. They quickly become proficient at changing the furniture arrangement of the room to suit the lesson. After all, the purpose of installing movable furniture in city classrooms is to allow the teacher to change the physical environment of the classroom to fit different learning situations. Few teachers actually move the furniture during the course of the day. In the child-centered classroom, furniture rearranging is one of the orderly routines developed with the children. Housekeeping is another routine, so that the children actually do the work necessary to help the teacher move easily from one method to another.

Can a teacher deviate from the assigned curriculum and the traditional method of teaching without being misjudged or even negatively criticized by the principal or district superintendent? Suffice it to say here that entire school systems throughout the country are moving toward this method of education, and principals and district superintendents are reacting favorably and supportively toward teachers who are willing to try it.

SELECTED READINGS

Books

ALMY, MILLIE. *Ways of Studying Children.* New York: Teachers College Press, 1959.

ASHTON-WARNER, SYLVIA. *Teacher.* New York: Bantam Books (NM4435), 1963.

BELTH, MARC. *The New World of Education.* Boston: Allyn & Bacon, 1970.

FROMME, ALLAN. *Our Troubled Selves.* New York: Pocket Books (671–77034–095), 1967.

FUCHS, ESTELLE. *Teachers Talk.* Doubleday (Anchor A668), 1969.

JERSILD, ARTHUR J. *When Teachers Face Themselves.* New York: Teachers College Press, 1955.

MOUSTAKAS, CLARK. *The Authentic Teacher.* Cambridge, Mass.: Howard A. Doyle, 1966.

ORNSTEIN, A., and VAIRO, P., eds. *How to Teach Disadvantaged Youth.* New York: David McKay, 1969.

STANDING, E. M. *Maria Montessori: Her Life and Work.* New York: Mentor Books (MQ425), 1962.

11 The Key That Opens Up Classrooms

THE ROLE OF THE ADMINISTRATOR

Remember the story of Willie Sutton and his single-minded purposiveness? With that same attitude, we educators (parents, teachers, and administrators) want to keep foremost in our minds that the child is the principal agent in the learning process. Our united efforts are to help the child reach his highest potential insofar as each of us, in our proper role, can do so. The role of the elementary-school administrator is our concern here, but only in so far as the method we are advocating is involved. It is not our purpose to write a treatise on the role of the administrator in the overall educational process. The central question with which we are here concerned is, How can the elementary-school administrator most effectively fulfill his role in the program we are proposing in this book?

The suggestions we will make in answer to this question are the result of our working with community school district superintendents and their staffs. We pass on these suggestions with the hope that they will not only prevent avoidable errors but will foster constructive, cooperative action, for without it no method can achieve its maximum potential. Certainly the generous cooperation we received from the school administrators with whom we worked accounts in large measure for the success of the program.

Not a few school administrators throughout the United States have publicly supported the general type of education we are promoting. Innovations of this kind (the Open School method, the Integrated Day method, the Modified British Informal School method) have been introduced to various schools across the country. In the area we know best, the New York City metropolitan area, an increasingly large number of school administrators have expressed their desire to initiate our program in their elementary schools. Of course, we are very pleased with the administrative support we have received. But what about the administrators who are not familiar with this program—what do we expect of them? In the first instance, we expect only a minimal positive reaction—that is, that they consider this program not as a necessary replacement of the traditional method, but as an alternative method of teaching for at least some of their teachers.

The contention sometimes made that everything in the more traditional and formal method of teaching is obsolete or ineffective is, we believe, frivolous and irresponsible. Good teachers employing the more traditional method have been and still are successful in varying degrees. The more traditional method has some time-tested techniques that are still valuable for many purposes. However, recent discoveries in developmental psychology, which have been tested enough to warrant their confident use, give us alternate ways of capturing interests, sustaining motivation, and developing personal learning styles in the child. It is not a question of supplanting the old with the new, the ineffective with the effective, the bad with the good. The question is, rather, how we shall retain the best of the traditional methods while incorporating the best of the new test findings.

There is also the question of the teacher's individual style of teaching. We all recognize that teachers have individual personalities—hence, individual teaching styles. A method with which one teacher feels comfortable, one that permits him to reach a high potential as a teacher, might be the ruin of another person. Some teachers may feel more comfortable and may do their most effective teaching only with the more traditional method. Others may require the more informal method we are proposing. Still others may feel most comfortable with a method that makes use of each to attain different objectives. We think it is very unwise to require a teacher to use any method but the one he is convinced is best for him.

Granted these premises, it is our conclusion that teachers who are convinced that not all of the elements of the more traditional and formal teaching are successful for their pupils should be allowed an option. If they are convinced that they have found an alternative method that will make their teaching more effective, that will make the learning process a more joyous and rewarding one for the children, then they should be given the freedom to adopt it. Administrators fulfill one of the requirements of their role when they grant freedom to teachers to use the teaching style that each finds most worthwhile.

The correlative of this is also part of the administrator's role: while granting reasonable freedom to the teacher regarding his teaching style, the administrator must exercise his responsibility to make sure that the method chosen by the teacher does not result in poorer education for the children in his class. Certainly no alternative method should be required to produce within a year demonstrably better results than the more traditional method in order for a principal to allow teachers to use it. The fact that the traditional method continues to be used without significant changes in a given school is no reason for prohibiting a method that would prove to be at least equally effective. Given time, the newer method might prove to be more effective. But how is one to know until it is tried?

The environmental method is not proposed as a panacea for all educational problems. There is no one method that is perfectly suited to all teachers, all pupils, or all circumstances. One method may work best under one set of circumstances, while another may be best under different circumstances. Not infrequently, one teacher may get best results by using different methods at different times to accomplish specific goals. Furthermore, children exposed to various methods have a better chance of finding their best learning style. We do not think that our method is a miraculous process whereby people who are proven failures as teachers can be transformed into good, much less excellent, teachers. We do not promise that every teacher who tries this method will automatically succeed with it. It is not "teacherproof."

We are convinced that our method is better, generally speaking, than the exclusive use of the more traditional method, but this does not mean that the school administrator has to think so. Burdened with the responsibility of protecting the best interests of the pupils—a burden teachers also bear—we understand the desire of the administrator to prevent an untried or educationally unsound program from upsetting the educational process of the children. All we ask of him is that he consider the method proposed here with an open mind, as an alternative method to be introduced under the proper circumstances with his approval and support. Let him try it as a pilot program in one classroom if he so desires. But one thing is certainly predictable: unless the principal of the school in which it is initiated is convinced from the start of its validity as an alternative method, and gives it his sincere approval and support, the odds are high that it will be foredoomed to failure.

Lack of support on the part of the principal can kill any new program in a school. Principals have the task of preserving the best elements in the more traditional methods while supporting promising innovations, if they wish to be true to their obligations. They must not deprive any teacher or any child of help that might come from any legitimate source in the educational world. They must understand alternative methods of teaching in order to judge the merits of each and to decide whether or not they will support an orderly and measured trial of the one (s) they deem to be educationally sound.

At workshops we have heard teachers say that they intend to introduce our method of teaching into their classrooms clandestinely, in spite of their principal "who is against any change." No teacher should attempt to use this method without the explicit knowledge and consent of the principal or the staff member clearly charged with the responsibility for supervising instruction in the school. A deliberately secretive or defiant attitude on the part of the teacher militates against the open, warm, sharing, and cooperative atmosphere required for this method in the classroom. With the approval and support of the principal, the teacher can be relaxed and secure enough to give the method the full attention it needs to succeed. For this reason, teachers who plan to initiate this program into their classrooms should first discuss the matter with their principal. But no principal should be expected to give his approval unless the method is explained clearly to him (or a copy of this book is loaned to him to read).

What does a teacher do when the principal refuses even to listen to any new suggestions? This teacher should explore the possible avenues of bringing this problem to the district superintendent for his action on the matter. Failing that, he should act in and through a teachers' association or teachers' union to confront administrators who refuse to respond fairly to the legitimate interests of teachers.

It is expected that if some teacher in his school approaches a principal who is not acquainted with the method proposed in this book, he will give the teacher a fair hearing. It is the principal's role to know what the teacher intends to do and how he plans concretely to initiate the program and to develop it in an orderly way. Only then can the principal respond intelligently and discuss whether or not the method should be initiated in that particular school, or at that particular time, or by that particular teacher. Sometimes a teacher who is most enthusiastic about anything new is the least competent to initiate even the soundest of programs. It is our experience that the program is best introduced by a teacher with proven classroom ability and discipline control who is also quite sure of where he is going and how he plans to get there. Therefore we think it is the role of the administrator to make the final decision after discussing whether or not the program should be introduced into the school, and who should introduce it.

Once the principal has granted his approval and decided who should initiate it and how it should be initiated, he must try to give the teacher all the support necessary to make the program a success. There are many ways in which the principal can help: Almost always there are materials buried away in various closets or storerooms of the school building that can be used profitably, and these should be made easily available. Small amounts of money may be needed sometimes to get the program started, and the principal should try to cut through the red tape and make this money readily available. (Any teacher who makes many or unreasonable demands either does not understand the method or wants done by others that which he should be doing himself.) During the early stages of the program, visits to the classroom show the teacher and pupils the principal's interest and encouragement and are extremely helpful. If through his own understanding of the method the principal is able to offer, along with encouragement for what has been successfully accomplished by the teacher and children, positive suggestions for further developments, the program will mature rapidly. The authors have witnessed cases where the principals by their helpful classroom visitations have brought about extraordinary results with this program.

Let us reverse the situation: consider circumstances wherein the principal has a clear knowledge of the method and its objectives, and is convinced that it should be introduced into his school. (It has not been proposed by any teacher yet.) He envisions it, let us suppose, at least as a method of reaching a number of children in his school who are turned off by the more traditional approach. What steps should he take to fulfill his role, and at the same time allow the teachers to fulfill their role, in this enterprise?

The principal must make sure that no teacher is urged to initiate the program until he understands it quite thoroughly and has decided voluntarily that he wishes to put it into practice in his classroom. If teachers have had no previous experience in this method, they should have some workshop experience before attempting it. They too need the guidance of an experienced person when beginning it until they find themselves doing it comfortably.

Regarding the previous statement that no teacher should be coerced into using this method, it should be added: be wary of teachers, few though they may be, who go along with any request the principal makes (privately, they reveal, "for the sake of peace"). Their lack of genuine interest and serious intent will militate strongly against the success of this program.

It is very important to have an experienced person guide those inexperienced in this method. It is the role of the administrator (either the district superintendent or principal) to provide such an experienced person. We look upon the function of such a person not as an evaluator, critic, or even supervisor. In our workshop we have trained teachers for this position whom we call demonstration teachers. They work as colleagues with the classroom teachers when the latter are beginning to put this method into practice. We train demonstration teachers to perform this function because we learned from experience that most teachers (there are indeed notable exceptions) who are experienced in the traditional method of teaching cannot make the transition in an orderly and confident way from that method to the method described in this book without some initial on-the-spot assistance. Problems do not ordinarily arise from the theory of the method; rather, the step-by-step details of classroom management are the major source of difficulty. However, a good, experienced teacher who has mastered our suggestions on procedures would experience relatively little difficulty. Nevertheless, the psychological support in the knowledge that someone is available to help out in the transitional period is extremely comforting. Once the teacher develops sufficient practical skill and confidence, no help is needed.

In a school with no previous experience in the method, the principal should choose a teacher to initiate this program who has demonstrated clearly and over a period of time all the basic qualities of a superior teacher. With a modicum of assistance and a mastery of the material covered in this book, this teacher will quickly develop into a demonstration teacher. He will then be able to help others initiate the method in two ways: others could go to this teacher's classroom to observe how the method works in practice, and this demonstration teacher could, if someone temporarily cared for his pupils, go to the classroom of the novice to give on-the-spot assistance.

Every administrator knows that any good program can easily fail in the hands of a teacher who is basically a failure at teaching. We all know of teachers who fail miserably with any method of teaching they use. They simply are teachers in name, but not in fact. We discovered, however, that some teachers who were considered below average or just average while using the more traditional method, blossomed forth into very good teachers using our method. It is folly to allow a poor teacher to initiate any method, so such a teacher should not be allowed to initiate this method. A principal would be taking a chance with a below-average teacher. An average teacher might do a superior job of initiating the method, but there is no prior evidence. Therefore, it is wiser to have a reliable superior teacher start the program. If such a teacher is enthusiastic about starting it and has done the necessary preparatory work, the outcome can be forecasted with a very high probability of success.

Many of the suggestions offered so far to principals apply, with certain changes, to district superintendents or their assistant superintendents in charge of curriculum and teaching. Our experience with this level of administration has been very pleasant. We received a full and fair hearing followed by approval and support, but again, we cannot emphasize enough the necessity of communicating clearly in terms of detailed classroom procedures exactly what one intends to do. No district superintendent or his responsible delegate will give approval and support to an innovative program simply because it seems to be appealing and is new. He must have a reasonable guarantee of its educational soundness grounded on verified data and tried with at least satisfactory results in comparable schools. A teacher should not feel offended or put upon if requested to supply such solid substantiation. It is the administrators' role to protect the children within his community school district.

Principals who initiate this program in their schools should apprise the district superintendent of this fact. Furthermore, not only should all the members of the principal's supervisory staff be aware of such an innovation and understand it, but an effort should be made to acquaint the district coordinators with the program. When these suggestions are followed, this program can work cooperatively with other programs in the school and in the district. Progressive math programs, reading projects, and individualized instruction can be programmed to coincide nicely with our program. The administrator on any level who keeps all of his supervisory and teaching personnel communicating well, coordinating their activities well, is assured of an efficient operation. Fortunately, in most of the districts with which we have worked, our program was integrated with other special programs because all of us worked together. Knowing how effective this is, we can only urge administrators who would like to incorporate this program into their schools or districts to follow the same procedure. It takes a number of organizational meetings to bring this about, but it most assuredly pays off in high dividends.

The educational administrator was first, and must always remain at heart, a teacher; otherwise, he would not be an effective educational administrator. He should know all that a teacher has to know about our method. Only in this way will he be able to help both his teachers and his pupils best. As a leader, he must grasp new ideas and new methods and initiate the method that promises substantial success. The overall responsibility belongs to the administrator; his function is to know and help all the others in the educational process to fulfill their individual roles as best they can.

12 Happy to Help

THE ROLE OF THE COMMUNITY

In the past, one of the main criticisms of the large public school systems was that they were vast impersonal bodies insensitive to the needs of individual communities. Critics deplored the fact that the community played no definite role in the choice of educational materials and personnel and in the actual job of educating the children. Decentralization was supposed to correct these faults, but in reality, very little change has taken place. Parents and other qualified adults are now able to elect members of the community school boards, who in turn decide upon educational policies and programs. Little else has been done to actually bring the people of the community into the day-to-day educational process. If one of the purposes of education is to prepare the child to take his place in the community and to act as an agent of change in his community, then it is vital that the community contribute to the education of its children. We believe that our method of education requires and invites more community participation than the teacher-centered formal method, which centers entirely too much on one person, the teacher.

In our method, the community has many roles, and it would be helpful to examine them one by one. In the "Role of the Teacher," (chapter 10) we stated that the teacher is the greatest *single* resource person in the child's educational experience. Similarly, the child's immediate community is the greatest *collective* resource body for elementary learning. Once past the stage of infancy, the child's first contacts are with his immediate neighborhood. His mother takes him with her to the food store, the shoe-repair store, and the bank. He sees cars and trucks on the street. The physical manifestations of his immediate neighborhood become as familiar to him as those of his own home. His neighborhood is also full of people. Each building, each store, each street holds a potential motivation for learning, if the knowledges and special talents of the people in the community are used wisely. If a survey of a given neighborhood were to be taken, various talents would be discovered in the arts, the professions, domestic skills, construction skills, and so on. The children themselves might interview parents and neighbors or conduct a talent search for particular skills in one apartment building. This reservoir of skills could be used to supplement the teacher's expertise in various ways. Some adults are willing to come into a classroom and work with the children. Others, who put in long hours at work or are ill at ease in a classroom, may just demonstrate a particular skill to the teacher, who can then pass it on to her children.

In one sixth-grade class, a mother came in to show the children how to make puppets from rolls of gauze and plaster of Paris, which is normally used to put casts on broken bones. The puppets were used for a representation of how people lived in ancient China. In a fourth-grade class, a father shared his expertise in photography with a group of interested children. A busy dentist came to school on Friday, his day off, to help a group of children who were constructing a model of the human head. A third-grader's aunt showed the teacher how to make tiny artificial flowers from tissue paper for a group of children who were adding a medieval garden to the medieval castle constructed by another group. We could go on and on with examples of community people who gave freely and willingly of their time and who were delighted to be called upon.

Our environmental method of education is flexible and can work around the busy schedules of community people. A group of fifth-grade children became interested in foods and were researching the origins of their favorite foods. They were able to leave the classroom at 9 A.M. and go with a school aide to the local fruit store to interview the proprietor before the store got too busy with customers. The teacher did not have to worry that they were missing reading or arithmetic. Important things were going on in the classroom as other children worked on various projects, but the important discoveries of all would be discussed and shared at some future time. The "food" group was free to pursue a chosen interest and to participate in a total learning experience. At the same time, the community was also actively contributing to the children's education. This constant interrelationship between child and community helps to produce a more community-minded adult, an adult more aware of his responsibilities toward the betterment of his own community.

We stated in previous chapters that this method of education uses many materials to give the child many concrete experiences. The people of the community can play an important role in collecting and finding materials. It has often been said, particularly in the antique business, that "one man's garbage is another man's treasure." This saying also holds true in environmental education. Even the busiest mother, with many children and an outside job, can save the cardboard rollers from paper goods, wire hangers, or egg cartons. In this small but tangible way she participates in the education of her children. Storekeepers in the community, if asked, have proved willing to save many things formerly consigned to the junk heap: clean cartons, Styrofoam packing, scraps of cloth and leather, bits of wood, and so on. Junk, yes, but invaluable aids to construction, experimentation, discovery, and discussion in the classroom.

Our country has often been criticized for its throwaway psychology. Solid waste disposal is an enormous problem. One side effect of our efforts might be a generation of children trained to be more frugal with materials who will thereby help to alleviate the waste-disposal problem. A group of fifth-graders was able to collect fourteen differently shaped glass containers, all designed to contain a quart of liquid. Their question was, "Why can't all bottles used to contain one quart of liquid be the same?" They would certainly be easier to pack and store, easier for the consumer to recognize, and could be collected and recycled by several different companies interchangeably. They wrote letters to various companies and are awaiting answers.

As more and more teachers become proficient in this approach, there will be a demand for more and more materials. Organizations within the community looking for worthwhile projects could certainly direct part of their efforts toward collecting materials that are needed in the classrooms, thereby actively helping the schools in the community. A byproduct of this kind of relationship would be an increase in communication between the schools and the people in the community. Teachers would become aware of the many resources they could call upon, and community people would have more knowledge of what is actually going on in the classroom, thereby satisfying the needs of both groups.

At the beginning of each school year, it is poignant to watch the mothers bring their kindergarten-age children to school for the first time. They come proudly, yet reluctant to entrust their most precious possessions to the tender mercies of the teachers and the other children. It soon becomes evident that the parent's chief concern is with the child's physical welfare during school hours. A parent is quick to protest when a child's physical well-being is threatened. Too many parents are slow to question what is being done to their child's mind and spirit. It is incumbent upon the community to be informed not only of what is going on in a particular classroom, but also to be informed about new ideas in education. This sounds like a tall, impossible order. "People are much too busy," it is agreed, to read educational tomes and pronouncements, even if they are sufficiently interested. Many people do not have the educational background to interpret what they read about new methodology. Why not trust the "experts" to concern themselves with the education of the children? They should trust the experts to some extent, but an informed community is a helpful community, and a participating community cannot help but be informed. Moreover, there are several ways in which busy parents can become better informed about educational matters.

Teachers working with our approach to education have themselves been able to open their classrooms to visitors without disturbing the educational process and without putting undue strain upon themselves. Visitors to an open classroom are regarded as interested adults and are soon drawn into projects by the children. The children are delighted to have an audience to explain their projects and goals to, and the children do not hesitate to ask for ideas or advice. (In a sixth-grade classroom, one of the authors found herself in a discussion with a group of boys about where to run the railroad in their model of a pollution-free city. They listened politely to her arguments but did not accept her route.) By actually visiting classrooms, the people of the community can better understand the psychology behind the informal classroom method and can actually see the enthusiasm of children pursuing their own learning.

Another way for the community to become informed is through conferences with the teacher. All too often these parent-teacher conferences are a pointless waste of time, especially if the child is an average child in a formal classroom. The child blends in as part of the total group, and the teacher has little to say about the particular individual. In our method, the teacher deals with every child on a one-to-one basis and gets to know the unique characteristics of each child. If the parent comes to the conference with specific questions and problems, then the conference is valuable to both parent and teacher. The parent gains insight into the method of education and how her particular child is progressing, and the teacher gains insight into the child's homelife and how it influences the child's performance. An informed parent and a concerned teacher can then work jointly to adjust their goals for the child so that these goals realistically meet the child's needs and abilities.

The parents' associations and the community school boards play a vital role in keeping the community informed. It is their job to accumu-

late, read, and digest what is important and current in the field of education. They must then take this information and present it to the parents
in a palatable and understandable form through school newspapers,
newsletters, periodic bulletins, and notices sent home with the children.
The parents' associations and community school boards should be the
town criers of the community, broadcasting the educational news to all
who will listen. Too many people in the community are made to feel
outside the tightly closed circle of the parents' association executive
board. Perhaps more people would be drawn in if a greater effort were
made to keep them better informed.

At this point, Wave Hill is conducting a series of slide lectures at
parents' association meetings, using pictures taken in the actual classrooms and explaining the techniques and results of using the method.
The lecture is then described in the school newspaper so that those
unable to attend may be reached. School newspapers are all too often a
combination of two elements: reports on past and future happenings,
and ads for local merchants. Every school newspaper should have a
column in every issue concerned with current trends in education. School
newspapers are a useful tool for keeping the community informed.

All schools send some type of report to parents at periodic inter-
vals, but how many schools give parents the opportunity to evaluate the
progress made by the children? During our summer program of 1970 we
sent evaluation questionnaires to all the parents involved. It contained
questions such as:

1. (a) My child liked the program   ☐
   (b) My child did not like the program   ☐
2. (a) My child learned a little   ☐
   (b) My child learned a lot   ☐
   (c) My child learned nothing   ☐
3. (a) As a parent, I think this program helped my child very much   ☐
   (b) As a parent, I think this program did not help my child   ☐
   (c) As a parent, I think this program could have helped my child
       more   ☐
4. What did you like most about the program?
5. What did you like least about the program?
6. What suggestions do you have to make the program a better one?

The questionnaire also included a checklist of specific questions.

Directions: Please circle Yes or No for the following statements regarding
your child since he joined the Wave Hill program.

1. My child is better able to work with   Yes ☐ No ☐
   other children.
2. My child talks more to me and to the family   Yes ☐ No ☐
   about himself.

3. My child is better able to think of something   Yes ☐ No ☐
   worthwhile to do that is new and different
   for him/her.

4. My child seems better able to start something and   Yes ☐ No ☐
   finish it without much help.

The questionnaire not only enables parents to participate in the evaluation of their child's progress; it also makes parents realize that there are ways other than numerical or letter grades to evaluate their child's growth. Perhaps the alternative ways tell a more complete story.

The TV news media and the press give extensive coverage to student riots, attacks upon teachers, and diatribes against the educational community itself. The local community can exert a great deal of pressure upon the media to balance this fare with accounts of worthwhile educational programs in the schools. There are many more worthwhile educational programs than there are riots and attacks.

We are all agreed that individual communities should assume a greater role in the decentralized community schools. Our method of education makes this possible because it uses both the material and the human resources of the community, and it builds an informed community by way of informal visits to schools, parent-teacher conferences, parents' associations, community school boards, and community publications.

SELECTED READINGS

Books

CUBAN, LARRY. *To Make a Difference*. New York: Free Press, 1970.

FRIEDENBERG, EDGAR Z. *Coming of Age in America*. New York: Vintage Book (V368), 1967.

GINOTT, HAIM G. *Between Parent and Child*. New York: Avon Books (W139), 1969.

HOMAN, WILLIAM E. *Child Sense*. New York: Basic Books, 1969.

MUSSEN, P.; CONGER, J.; and RAGAN, J. *Child Development and Personality*. 3d ed. New York: Harper & Row, 1969.

13 The Scarecrow's Brain, the Tinman's Heart, and the Lion's Courage

HOW TO BEGIN

When asked what is needed to put the environmental method into practice, we can only think of *The Wizard of Oz*. Three things are really needed: the scarecrow's brain, the tinman's heart, and the lion's courage. The scarecrow's brain represents the understanding and the know-how. The tinman's heart symbolizes the willingness to open one's heart and mind in the classroom. The lion's courage may be the most important of all: someday you must begin. Then, of course, there is always the magic of the glass slippers. A little magic, which may be trust in yourself and in your children, always goes a long way.

There are probably as many ways to begin as there are teachers. Every teacher is encouraged to tailor the program to suit his own personality and classroom style. However, we have found through experience in many classrooms that a certain sequence seems to work best for the majority of classes. Within the sequence, there is great flexibility.

The first step in the sequence is to plan carefully for the selection of materials and for the organization of the children. Questions the teacher must ask himself in the planning stage are: How many groups can I handle comfortably? What materials will interest my children and are on their level of operation? What materials are readily available? What do I hope that the children will accomplish through the use of the materials? What specific outcomes do I anticipate? These questions must be dealt with carefully and concretely, so the teacher can set the outer limits for his initial experiences. Once he has selected his turn-on agents and other objects to group with them, he is ready to start operations within the framework of his planned conclusions. Mrs. Smith, for example, will work in this method three hours per week with a prepared list of math and science materials, hoping that through the use of these specific aids the children will make discoveries in fractional parts and in magnetism. Mrs. Smith is now ready to begin.

The second step in the sequence is to systematically help your children develop a working relationship with manipulative materials. This development, too, allows for great latitude. One teacher may start out with a single, limited interest area, and help four children at a time in its use. Another teacher may attempt to involve the entire class at once. We have found the whole-class method infinitely more successful for many reasons. Many children refuse to work productively at prosaic jobs while others are being exposed to something new and fascinating, even though they have been assured of their turn. Sometimes the new activity is noisy and distracting in an otherwise still classroom. It is most helpful with children of all ages to start off with a short discussion involving the entire class. The teacher may say, "I am going to allow you to play with, work with, or discover with the materials I have in this box. Before I show them to you, tell me, what are your responsibilities toward these materials?"

In every classroom, we have been able to elicit from the children that their responsibilities toward the materials are to take care of them, to clean up when they are finished, and to share. We ask the children to count the pairs of hands belonging to the teachers. It is obviously an easier task for everyone to participate in cleanup. It is sufficient in the children's first exposure to go through the routines of choosing a material, playing with it for a short time, cleaning up, and perhaps ending with a group evaluation of their performance, their feelings, and their problems.

Each subsequent time that the materials are used, a new element should be added. The second exposure might define routines for changing materials and provisions for the children to move about easily from group to group. This too needs discussion, demonstration, and acting out, so that children learn to work together harmoniously.

At about the third or fourth session, it is wise to introduce the responsibility for recording what the children have accomplished. There are many reasons for keeping records and these reasons can be explored with the class. How will the teacher be made aware of what everyone is doing? How can the child remember what he did last time? How can he share his discoveries with his classmates? The recording should take many forms: an individual log, a cooperative story, a chart, a graph, a picture, a diagram, a poem, a script, and a shoebox movie are all acceptable, desirable ways of keeping records. The important thing is that the children should be made aware that they are responsible for contributing to the record of their own progress.

At the same time that the children are developing a relationship to materials, other things should be happening. First, the teacher should be noting through careful observation the kinds of materials that will be successful turn-on agents for her particular children. With younger children, observation is the key. Do the boys collect and trade bubble-gum cards? Do the girls bring little dolls to school? With older children, letting them express their preferences by means of a question sheet might be very useful. During these early exposures to materials, it is helpful to let children share their accomplishments quite often; children stimulate and motivate each other. It is also profitable at times to zero in on a particular object, such as a geoboard, and throw the discussion open to the entire class. "What are some of the things we can explore with the geoboard?"

Problems with this method will be starting to crop up and should be dealt with as they arise. What do we do about the rising noise level? Can we choose two children at each session who will be responsible for monitoring the noise level and telling us by some prearranged signal—cutting the lights or ringing a bell—that the room is getting too noisy?

What do we do about the disruptive child who sets out to deliberately destroy materials? Can we expose him to this informal method for short periods of time until he develops enough self-control to participate? Should he choose a buddy who will help him by way of friendly reminders? Could a group of children take on the task of including him and helping him? If all else fails, could he possibly be removed from the classroom during the initial experiences, so that the others may develop their routines, and be returned when all are secure enough to cope with him?

What do we do about children who do not participate in cleanup? Is peer pressure sufficient to handle this problem, or must the teacher intervene? Who are the children who only work alone and who do not relate at all to their peers? How can we help them to socialize and enjoy group experiences?

What do we do about the child who flits aimlessly from group to group without ever really accomplishing anything? We might set up a series of tasks for this child with short-term involvement and assured success to build up his confidence. Flitting children usually lack self-confidence or have a great fear of failure. They feel that if they don't become involved, they can't fail. If the child comes to learn that error is a very positive experience in this method, perhaps he won't be so fearful of trying.

There are probably as many ways of dealing with these problems as there are different classes in a school, but many of them should be dealt with in the initial encounters before you commit a large portion of your school day to this approach. When you can answer yes to the question Have my children learned to use materials neatly, economically, and profitably? you are ready for the next step.

The third step in the sequence will entail some physical rearrangement of your room so that you have space to set up interest areas. If you feel it necessary to retain all the furniture in the room, the materials for each interest area may be contained in a large carton and set up on tables during each work period. Cleanup would consist of placing the materials into the proper cartons. As a beginner, limit the physical setup to four interest areas. Remember, as you select your turn-on agents, that the materials in these areas can be used for many different purposes and projects. Set very definite times and routines for using the centers. Make sure the materials selected are interesting and meaningful to the children. Clearly specify what is expected of the children. Your expectations may vary from the very simple short-term use of a single interest center for the child who is finding out how many different kinds of triangles he can make on a geoboard, to a complicated long-term project combining the materials in all the interest centers to build a model of Apollo 14.

When you plan your centers, think first of the interests and levels of operation of your children, but think also of the curriculum goals for your grade. Certain interest areas are basic to all grades and to all projects. The children will need a center where they can find many tools for measurement, both standard and nonstandard. Bottles and jars of many sizes, teaspoons, rulers, tapes, string, trundle wheels, protractors, stopwatches, timers, and clocks and thermometers of all kinds are vital components of this center. Their uses are learning experiences in themselves and they are valuable aides in other explorations.

What we like to call a junk collection is a useful center in every classroom. It might contain the following: paper, cardboard, scraps of cloth, leather, wood, plastics, spools, paper-towel rollers, buttons, scissors, paste, toothpicks, spools, old wrapping paper, and greeting cards. These are some of the materials necessary for creative art work, building models, and creating and clothing puppets. These two centers, one for measuring tools and the other for "junk," are considered basic to every classroom, and they should be replenished throughout the school year.

Other centers may vary according to the interests of the children, the goals of the teacher, the seasons of the year, or the events of the world. An interest in scientific experimentation might lead to a center stocked with materials needed for exploration of the properties of air, or one stocked with bones and artifacts. Another center might be filled only with materials found out-of-doors and brought back for further investigation. A fifth-grade class whose social studies unit studied different geographic locations were hard at work setting up dry-land and wet terrariums. This interest led to expansion in two directions and the need for more room. One group became interested in planting, so they set up a series of experiments. The other group investigated animals that would live in a dry area and became involved with animals, and they soon had a sizable collection of animals on loan in the classroom. A living science center was created and remained as long as the children's interest held out; it was eventually replaced by a puppet theater and a surge of interest in dramatics.

The separation of materials into centers has two purposes. First, in order to exist in a classroom, we must have some logical method for finding things and putting them away. Everything must have a place. Second, many times the very grouping of related materials acts as a turn-on agent and suggests to the child explorations in which he might become involved. However, materials may be taken from one center to another and may be combined to carry out a project. When it is time for cleanup, the children should be able to put materials in their proper place easily and quickly.

As we have said before, certain materials or interest areas are basic to the classroom and basic to all explorations, while others need frequent changing or dismantling to make room for a new interest. Many times it is only necessary to find new turn-on agents because the same "junk" materials can be used to construct the model of Apollo, build a medieval village, create a model pollution-free city, or make an art object. The same scales can be used to weigh an animal or to estimate how many beans there are in the jar.

The fourth step in the sequence is continuous and consistent evaluation of the children's progress. We have already stated that sharing is an important part of the child's total accomplishment. There is a danger here that both the teacher and the child's peers will accept and praise all accomplishments that are self-initiated and independently done. This must not be allowed to take place. We are interested in building the youngster's self-image, but it must be a valid buildup, or it may soon collapse. In many instances we must save our praise for a very real accomplishment and spur a youngster on with questions like How could we make this better? and What does this need before we can say it is finished? Let us now explore some of the elements that the teacher and the class are jointly evaluating.

There must be periodic evaluations of the total program and of its effectiveness in meeting the needs of all the children. Many times, a day in which many things seem to go wrong is a good time to call your group together and explore the reasons for chaotic performance, dropping off of interest, and antisocial behavior. Many insights can be gained from discussion with the children, and they often have good ideas for improving the smoothness of the operation. It might be necessary to change an interest center, reorganize the furniture in the room, or rethink various routines. Discussing these things with your children is another indication· of the very positive values of "failure."

Every child should be evaluated on a weekly basis. This is not as awesome as it sounds. It simply means that in the course of the week the teacher gets to each child and finds out just what he is doing, what his needs are, and what his goals are. By the end of the week, she knows which children are getting lost in the shuffle, which children need specific skills, and which children are potential leaders or buddies for less apt children. He might learn that Bill's only interest is science, and that Mary would, if left alone, create collages all week. The teacher's special tasks for the next week are emerging clearly. First, investigate possibilities for turning on and helping the lost children. Perhaps a buddy or inclusion in a well-organized group will help. Next, provide scheduled time for small group instruction in the needed skills and prepare materials for their drill and reinforcement. Assign Bill and Mary to specific tasks in other areas and check to see that they are completed. Try to use Mary's collection of collages as a steppingstone to math, reading, and creative writing. Meet with small groups to discuss how children can help each other. Set reasonable goals for getting around to the children so that you do not operate in a frenzy. Your relaxed, orderly attitude in proceeding from one to the other will help the children develop trust and patience. Every ten minutes that you spend alone with a single child or with a small group is worth infinitely more, we find, than the time you spend in the front of the room talking to the entire class.

An essential element in good evaluation is a sequential system of recording. The first recording that you do will probably be in the form of flow charts as described in chapter four of part one—to facilitate your planning and selection of materials. These charts should state your goals clearly. The second type of record is the weekly record for the individual child. These may be kept on individual cards or in a notebook:

JONES, JOHN   Week of Feb. 22–26

Projects worked on—puppet stage construction, puppets, script

Skills involved—planning, measuring, use of tools, creative writing—read *Little Indian Basket Maker*

Instruction received—use of yardstick, vocabulary for play about Indians— new vocabulary_____

Drill and check—equivalents, feet, inches, yards—vocabulary.

The third type of record would be a monthly overview of the projects that grew out of the turn-on agents. A comparison of this record with the original flow charts would give you a good indication of whether or not you are meeting the grade goals.

In some classes the teachers endeavor to insure that there is a record of every large completed project in the class reference library, so that it can be referred to throughout the year. At the end of the year, the class library might contain a film on the care of a guinea pig, an instruction manual on how to construct a model Apollo, a picture story of the development of the automobile, and a collection of art treasures of Class 3–206. Looking further, you might find a pattern book of dolls' clothes, a history in graphs of the class growth in spelling, a charming book of leaves with a story about each one, a set of scripts for the puppet theater, and a group of acetates showing common birds indigenous to New York might round out the collection. These are all examples from actual classrooms, and for the children they are permanent records of having passed through certain experiences. The class library becomes a living, growing thing, and books take on a new dimension for the child.

Perhaps you are now ready to start opening up your classroom, to start experimenting with materials and projects, and are held back only by fear of what might go wrong. Focus upon the worst possible initial try that you could experience: unbearable noise, misuse, destruction and theft of materials, aimless fooling around, breakdown of discipline, and utter chaos. Not a very pretty picture, and admittedly a very extreme one.

Now think in terms of why children are sent to school for ten out of twelve months every year. Children come to school to learn subject matters, how to live, how to cope with their immediate environment, how to relate to others, and how other cultures live and relate. If the children in your class have an initial experience as extreme as the one described above, then certainly their education up to this point has been lacking in certain basic elements, and it is certainly time to think about filling in the gaps. Perhaps the very thing that these children need is practice in social interaction. Furthermore, the disastrous initiation gives the teacher a blueprint for action in future experiences, and each of the areas of failure should be worked at and corrected.

Our primary aim is to develop in the child the ability to recognize a problem or situation, to call upon all his resources to help solve it, to know where to get help, and to come to some logical conclusion. After many avenues have been explored, the conclusion in some cases may very well be that a particular task is beyond the child's scope. The value of this for his future life, however, is incalculable. The child leaves school with the knowledge of how to go about solving real problems, and he knows which problems he needs outside help to solve.

With an ample share of the scarecrow's brain, the tinman's heart, and the lion's courage, the teacher need not be afraid to begin or to fail. The brain will help him to operate, the heart will carry him through, and the courage will enable him to turn failure into success.

Glossary

ALTERNATIVE METHOD: any method that can easily be used in conjunction with or instead of other methods of teaching, and is at least equally effective.

ANECDOTAL REPORTING: reporting that uses a subjective prose evaluation instead of numbers, letters, or symbols.

BRAINSTORMING: the process by which the teacher's mind is opened to freely associate in regard to an educational material or a learning situation, in order to explore as fully as possible where it can lead.

BRITISH INFANT SCHOOL METHOD: an interdisciplinary, child-centered, informal system of education practiced in the lower-grade schools of England for the whole or part of the day.

AGENT OF CHANGE: a person who is able to identify problems and to initiate constructive action to solve these problems.

CHILD-CENTERED METHOD: a psychology of education that regards the child as the initiator of his own learning at his own level of operation.

CUISENAIRE RODS: sets of colored wooden rods, calibrated in size to motivate the child's innate mathematical ability. The Cuisenaire rods concretely present the basic structures of arithmetic and elementary algebra. The name derives from their inventor.

DISCOVERY AREA: any portion of the classroom set up with manipulative materials and a place for children to work.

DISCOVERY PERIOD: the designated span of time in which children may work on their own at various projects.

ENVIRONMENTAL EDUCATION: a method of education that embraces two modern thrusts in education: the open classroom method and the concern for the environment.

EXPERIENCE CHART: a cooperative written record drawn from the experiences of the class.

EXPERIENCE LOG: a cooperative, ongoing written record of the children's explorations and discoveries during the discovery periods. This type of log is a useful recording device in the lower grades.

EXTERNAL DISCIPLINE: discipline imposed by the constant vigilance of the teacher.

FAMILY GROUPING: nongraded heterogeneous grouping that allows children to help one another.

FLOW CHART: the chart developed as a result of the brainstorming, grouping, and elimination process, to chart promising areas of exploration of materials. The chart may be used instead of a plan book by the teacher.

GEOBOARD: a square piece of plywood with a square (and/or circular) arrangement of pins. Colored rubber bands of various sizes are used with the board to make shapes, designs, and pictures.

HETEROGENEOUS GROUPING: placing children of varied levels of accomplishment in the same group.

HOMOGENEOUS GROUPING: grouping children according to reading levels.

INNOVATIVE: different from what exists at present.

INTEGRATED DAY: a school day that is combined into a whole with a minimum of timetabling. Within this day there is time and opportunity in a planned, educative environment for the social, intellectual, emotional, physical, and aesthetic growth of the child at his own rate of development.

INTERDISCIPLINARY LEARNING: learning that brings many knowledges, skills, and concepts to bear upon solving a relevant problem. Learning that is not categorized separately as math, science, reading, and so on.

INTEREST-GROUPS: groups formed because the members are all interested in working on the same project.

INTERNAL DISCIPLINE: control that the child himself develops to discipline his own behavior and to deal with situations himself. Its purpose is to select and use constructive behavior to accomplish desirable goals.

LOG: the written record kept by the child of his experiences during the discovery period; also, the record kept by the teacher of the weekly activities in the classroom.

MANIPULATIVE MATERIALS: objects with which the children can explore and work on projects; materials that are interesting in themselves or can be used to further a project.

MESS ABOUT: experiment or play with materials just to experience the nature of various substances.

OPEN CLASSROOM: a classroom set up in interest areas in which children can move freely from one area to another.

OPEN CORRIDOR: a system whereby children in an open classroom situation may also use the corridor for work and play.

PAN BALANCE: a balance scale made of heavy-duty plastic with two large pans to contain materials.

POP-IT BEADS: beads that can be taken apart and put back together easily. They are joined by individual fasteners.

PROJECTS: children's explorations; projects may vary from a half-hour's involvement to an entire week's involvement.

PROJECT GOALS: what the children are trying to accomplish, find out, learn, or build.

ROLE-PLAYING: acting out of various socializational and educational experiences with the purpose of discussing the roles of the various participants.

SHARING PERIOD: time or times during the day when children have the opportunity to share their discoveries and completed projects.

TANGRAM PUZZLES: an assortment of various pieces of plastic shapes that, when fitted together, form larger designated shapes; they lead easily to a study of angles.

TASK CARDS: cards, commercially or teacher-prepared, with suggested questions, projects, or areas of exploration.

TEACHER-CENTERED CLASSROOM: a classroom in which the teacher addresses the class as a whole most of the time, has the children occupy seats in consecutive rows, and almost continually controls the children's learning process.

TRADITIONAL METHOD: the method of education currently in use in most classrooms. (See above *teacher centered classroom*).

TRUNDLE WHEEL: a wheel, whose circumference usually measures a yard (although any size wheel could be employed), to which an arm is attached. It is used to have children visualize the relationships of linear and circular measurement, and radius, diameter, circumference. It may be homemade or purchased.

TURN-ON AGENTS: materials or situations sufficiently provocative to the children to motivate them to explore and learn.

VERTICAL GROUPING: nongraded or family grouping.

Index